A Comprehensive Guide

MULTIMEDIA JOURNALISM

Common Mistakes and Tips

OSMAN KARAKAS

About Book

Book Title: **Multimedia Journalism**

A Comprehensive Guide:

Subtitle: **Common Mistakes and Tips**

Format: Word/PDF

Size: 6X9 inches - 15.24X22.89 cm

Total Pages: 159

E-mail: okarakas@hotmail.com

Web: www.osmankarakas.com

CONTENTS

Preface:

Welcome to the world of "Multimedia Journalism: A Comprehensive Guide." In an era defined by digital innovation and rapid information dissemination, multimedia journalism stands at the forefront of modern storytelling. This book serves as a comprehensive resource for both aspiring multimedia journalists and seasoned professionals looking to enhance their skills.

The landscape of journalism has evolved dramatically in recent years. Traditional print journalism has been joined by a dynamic array of multimedia formats that include text, photos, videos, audio, interactive graphics, and more. Today's audiences expect news stories that not only inform but also engage and immerse them in the narratives. This book explores the tools, techniques, and principles that empower journalists to meet these expectations.

Our journey through the pages of this guide will take you on a captivating exploration of multimedia journalism's rich tapestry. We will delve into the art of storytelling, mastering the tools of the trade, navigating ethical considerations, and embracing emerging technologies that are reshaping journalism. Whether you're a student, a seasoned journalist, or simply an enthusiast of the craft, you will find valuable insights, practical tips, and inspiring case studies to elevate your multimedia journalism endeavors.

As we embark on this adventure together, we encourage you to embrace the spirit of innovation and curiosity that defines multimedia journalism. Our hope is that this book will not only equip you with the knowledge and skills to excel in the field but also inspire you to push the boundaries of storytelling, engage with your audience in new ways, and contribute to the ever-evolving world of journalism.

The field of multimedia journalism is dynamic, ever-changing, and filled with opportunities for those who are passionate about informing and engaging the world. So, let's begin this journey, armed with the tools and insights to craft compelling stories that resonate with our audiences in this digital age.

Happy reading and happy storytelling!

Osman Karakas

Author

Journalist & Lecturer

Chapter 1: Introduction to Multimedia Journalism

In this chapter, we'll explore the fundamental concepts of multimedia journalism and its significance in the modern media landscape.

Section 1.1: Defining Multimedia Journalism

Multimedia journalism is a dynamic field that seamlessly combines diverse forms of media to craft compelling and informative stories. In this section, we'll embark on a journey to dissect the essence of multimedia journalism, understanding both its definition and the profound reasons for its status as an indispensable component of contemporary journalism.

Multimedia journalism is more than just words on a page or a single photograph in a magazine. It's a multimedia symphony that harmoniously incorporates text, images, audio, video, and interactive elements to deliver news and stories with depth and impact.

In the digital age, where attention spans are fleeting and information overload is the norm, multimedia journalism stands as a beacon of innovation. It recognizes that people consume news in various ways, whether through reading articles, watching videos, listening to podcasts, or interacting with interactive graphics. By harnessing this diversity of media, multimedia journalism not only captures the audience's attention but also provides a more comprehensive understanding of complex stories.

At its core, multimedia journalism aims to engage, inform, and inspire. It leverages the power of visuals to evoke emotions, the clarity of audio to provide context, and the interactivity of digital platforms to encourage exploration. In doing so, it forges a profound connection between the storyteller and the audience.

As we progress through this book, you'll gain a deeper appreciation for the art and science of multimedia journalism. We'll explore the tools, techniques, and best practices that enable journalists to master this multifaceted craft. So, let's embark on this enlightening journey into the world of multimedia journalism, where words, images, sounds, and technology converge to create impactful narratives.

Section 1.2: The Importance of Multimedia in Modern Journalism

In today's digital age, multimedia elements have undergone a metamorphosis, profoundly altering the landscape of journalism. Elements such as photos, videos, and interactive graphics have transcended their supplementary roles to become integral components of news consumption. In this section, we will delve into the critical role played by multimedia in engaging audiences and conveying information effectively.

The integration of multimedia elements in journalism is a response to the changing preferences and behaviors of news consumers. Here's why it matters:

1. Enhanced Engagement:

Multimedia content has the remarkable ability to capture and sustain the audience's attention. A striking photograph, a poignant video clip, or an interactive map can draw readers into a story in ways that text alone cannot. When audiences are engaged, they are more likely to stay and explore the story, leading to a deeper understanding of the subject matter.

2. Visual Storytelling:

Humans are inherently visual beings. We process visual information much faster than text, making multimedia an ideal medium for storytelling. A well-chosen image or video can convey emotions, context, and nuances that words alone may struggle to express. Visual elements provide a visceral connection to the story, allowing readers to empathize with the subject matter.

3. Accessibility and Clarity:

Multimedia elements can simplify complex topics. Interactive graphics and diagrams can break down intricate concepts, making them accessible to a broader audience. Additionally, videos and audio recordings can provide firsthand accounts or interviews, adding depth and clarity to news reports.

4. Diversification of Content:

Multimedia journalism allows for versatility in content creation. Journalists can adapt their storytelling style to suit the subject matter. Whether it's a heart-wrenching video interview, a data-driven interactive piece, or a captivating photo essay, multimedia provides the tools to tailor content to the story's requirements.

5. Audience Reach:

Different people prefer different types of media. By incorporating multimedia elements, journalists can reach a more diverse audience. Some may gravitate towards videos on social media, while others prefer in-depth articles. Offering a variety of media formats increases the likelihood of connecting with a wider range of readers.

6. Virality and Shareability:

Multimedia content is highly shareable in the digital era. Compelling visuals or emotionally charged videos have the potential to go viral, spreading the message far beyond the initial readership. This amplification can turn a news story into a societal conversation.

In essence, multimedia journalism recognizes that modern audiences have varied preferences for how they consume news. By embracing multimedia, journalists not only cater to these preferences but also enrich the news narrative. As we progress through this book, we'll delve deeper into the techniques and strategies for harnessing the power of multimedia in your journalism endeavors.

Section 1.3: Evolution of Journalism in the Digital Age

In this section, we won't delve into the extensive historical aspects of journalism, but we will embark on a fascinating journey to explore the evolution of journalism within the context of the digital age. We'll examine how technological advancements have redefined the very essence of news production and consumption.

The digital age, often referred to as the Information Age, has ushered in profound changes in the journalism landscape. These changes can be summarized through several key points:

1. Digital Transformation:

The emergence of the internet and digital technologies marked a paradigm shift in journalism. News organizations transitioned from traditional print formats to digital platforms, allowing for real-time reporting and a global reach. The web became a new battleground for disseminating news, and newsrooms adapted to the 24/7 news cycle.

2. Citizen Journalism:

With the rise of smartphones and social media, ordinary individuals became active participants in the news ecosystem. Citizen journalists could capture and share news events as they unfolded, providing eyewitness accounts that traditional media couldn't always deliver. This shift democratized journalism, but it also raised questions about credibility and verification.

3. Interactivity and Engagement:

The digital age brought interactivity to news consumption. Readers could now comment on articles, participate in online polls, and engage in discussions through social media. This two-way communication transformed journalism from a one-sided transmission of information to a dynamic dialogue between news producers and consumers.

4. Multimedia Integration:

As we've discussed, multimedia elements became integral to storytelling. News articles were no longer limited to text; they could incorporate images, videos, infographics, and interactive features. This multimedia richness added depth and context to stories.

5. Data Journalism:

The digital age enabled the collection and analysis of vast amounts of data. Journalists began using data-driven storytelling techniques to uncover trends, patterns, and insights. Data journalism not only enhanced reporting but also fostered transparency and accountability.

6. Challenges and Ethics:

Alongside these advancements came challenges. The rapid dissemination of information on digital platforms made fact-checking and verification more critical than ever. Ethical dilemmas, such as the spread of misinformation and the erosion of privacy, emerged as pressing concerns.

7. Business Model Shifts:

Traditional revenue models for journalism, such as print advertising, faced disruption. News organizations explored new revenue streams, including digital subscriptions, sponsored content, and donations. These shifts had significant implications for the sustainability of journalism.

As we navigate through this book, you'll gain deeper insights into how these changes have shaped modern multimedia journalism. We'll explore the tools, strategies, and best practices that allow journalists to adapt and thrive in this evolving landscape, where technology continues to redefine the boundaries of storytelling and news dissemination.

Chapter 2: The Multimedia Journalist's Toolkit

In this chapter, we'll equip you with the essential tools and knowledge necessary to excel in the realm of multimedia journalism. Our journey begins with an exploration of the hardware that forms the foundation of your multimedia toolkit.

Section 2.1: Cameras, Microphones, and Other Equipment

As a multimedia journalist, your ability to capture high-quality visuals and audio is paramount. In this section, we will delve into the core components of your toolkit, including cameras, microphones, and other essential equipment that will empower you to tell compelling stories.

Cameras:

Cameras are your primary means of capturing images and videos. We'll discuss various types of cameras, from DSLRs to mirrorless cameras and even smartphone cameras. Each has its strengths and weaknesses, and we'll help you understand which is best suited for different situations.

DSLR Cameras: Renowned for their versatility and image quality, DSLR cameras offer manual control over settings, interchangeable lenses, and excellent low-light performance.

Mirrorless Cameras: These cameras combine the portability of a point-and-shoot with the flexibility of a DSLR. We'll explore their advantages in terms of size, weight, and innovative features.

Smartphone Cameras: The ubiquity of smartphones means you'll always have a camera at your disposal. We'll discuss how to maximize the potential of smartphone photography and videography.

Microphones:

Quality audio is as crucial as sharp visuals in multimedia journalism. We'll introduce you to various microphones and their applications.

Lavalier Microphones: These small, clip-on microphones are ideal for interviews and on-the-go reporting, ensuring clear and direct sound.

Shotgun Microphones: Shotgun mics are highly directional, capturing sound primarily from the front. They're ideal for reducing background noise in outdoor or crowded settings.

Handheld Microphones: Often used for field interviews or stand-up reporting, handheld microphones provide excellent audio quality and control.

Tripods and Stabilizers:

To maintain steady shots in both photography and videography, tripods and stabilizers are indispensable tools. We'll discuss the various options available and when to use them.

Lighting Equipment:

Proper lighting can make or break a multimedia production. We'll explore lighting kits, reflectors, and techniques for achieving professional-looking visuals.

Accessories and Gadgets:

From memory cards and external hard drives to smartphone gimbals and drone technology, we'll cover the accessories and gadgets that can enhance your multimedia journalism workflow.

By the end of this section, you'll have a solid understanding of the equipment at your disposal and how to select the right tools for each journalistic endeavor. Armed with this knowledge, you'll be well-prepared to embark on your multimedia storytelling journey, capturing and conveying stories with precision and impact.

Section 2.2: Software for Editing and Production

In the world of multimedia journalism, capturing compelling visuals and audio is only the beginning. To craft polished and engaging stories, you must also master the art of post-production. In this section, we'll explore the essential software tools used for editing and production in multimedia journalism.

Video Editing Software:

Video is a powerful medium for storytelling, and the choice of video editing software can significantly impact the quality of your multimedia productions. We'll delve into some of the most popular video editing tools used by multimedia journalists:

Adobe Premiere Pro: A professional-grade software known for its versatility and powerful editing features. It offers a wide range of tools for video and audio editing, color correction, and effects.

Final Cut Pro X: Apple's flagship video editing software, favored by many Mac users. It combines advanced features with an intuitive interface.

DaVinci Resolve: A free-to-use video editing software that also includes professional color grading tools. It's an excellent choice for journalists on a budget.

Audio Editing Software:

High-quality audio is crucial for multimedia journalism, especially for podcasts, interviews, and narration. We'll introduce you to audio editing software that ensures clear and professional sound:

Adobe Audition: Part of the Adobe Creative Cloud suite, Audition is a powerful audio editing tool that offers features for noise reduction, audio restoration, and multi-track editing.

Audacity: A free, open-source audio editing software known for its simplicity and accessibility. It's a great starting point for those new to audio editing.

GarageBand: If you're a Mac user, GarageBand provides a user-friendly platform for audio recording and editing, making it ideal for beginners.

Photo Editing Software:

In multimedia journalism, photo editing plays a crucial role in enhancing visual storytelling. We'll discuss photo editing software options to help you perfect your images:

Adobe Photoshop: The industry standard for photo editing, offering a wide range of tools for retouching, color correction, and image manipulation.

Lightroom: Another Adobe product, Lightroom is excellent for managing and enhancing large photo collections. It's particularly well-suited for photographers and photojournalists.

GIMP (GNU Image Manipulation Program): A free, open-source alternative to Photoshop, GIMP provides many advanced editing features.

Multimedia Production and Authoring Software:

Sometimes, multimedia journalists need to combine various media elements into interactive presentations or web-based stories. We'll explore software tools for multimedia production and authoring:

Adobe InDesign: Used for creating interactive PDFs and digital magazines, InDesign allows you to combine text, images, and multimedia elements seamlessly.

Visme: An online tool for creating interactive presentations and infographics, which can be embedded on websites or shared on social media.

StoryMapJS: A web-based tool for creating multimedia, interactive maps to enhance location-based storytelling.

By the end of this section, you'll have a comprehensive understanding of the software tools available to you for editing and producing multimedia content. These tools will empower you to refine and assemble your multimedia stories, ensuring they are polished, engaging, and ready to captivate your audience.

Section 2.3: Building a Multimedia Newsroom

Creating outstanding multimedia journalism requires more than just individual skills and equipment—it requires an environment that fosters collaboration, creativity, and efficiency. In this section, we will explore the key elements involved in building a multimedia newsroom that can thrive in the fast-paced world of journalism.

1. Defining Roles and Responsibilities:

A successful multimedia newsroom begins with a clear understanding of who does what. Journalists, photographers, videographers, editors, and digital producers all have distinct roles. Define these roles and responsibilities to ensure a smooth workflow.

2. Collaboration and Communication:

Effective communication is the backbone of any newsroom. Tools like project management software, instant messaging platforms, and regular team meetings help keep everyone informed and aligned on project goals and deadlines.

3. Multimedia Training:

Ensure that your team is well-versed in multimedia tools and techniques. Offer training sessions or access to resources that allow your journalists to continually improve their multimedia skills.

4. Equipment and Facilities:

Provide the necessary hardware and facilities for multimedia production. This includes camera equipment, recording studios, and editing stations. Regular maintenance and updates are essential to keep your tools in peak condition.

5. Content Management Systems (CMS):

Invest in a robust CMS that can handle multimedia content seamlessly. A good CMS allows for easy uploading, organization, and distribution of multimedia elements across various platforms.

6. Digital Asset Management (DAM):

Implement a DAM system to efficiently store, retrieve, and manage multimedia assets. This is especially crucial in newsrooms where large volumes of media are produced and reused.

7. Cross-Training:

Encourage cross-training among your team members. Journalists with multimedia skills and vice versa can fill in gaps during peak workloads and offer fresh perspectives.

8. Editorial Guidelines:

Develop clear editorial guidelines that cover multimedia content. This includes standards for image and video sourcing, captions, and multimedia ethics.

9. User-Friendly Workflows:

Streamline your production workflows to minimize bottlenecks. This might involve adopting agile project management methodologies or creating templates for common multimedia formats.

10. Adaptability and Flexibility:

The media landscape is ever-changing. Your newsroom must remain adaptable to new technologies and trends. Embrace experimentation and be open to evolving your processes.

11. Quality Control:

Establish quality control measures for multimedia content. This includes thorough editing, fact-checking, and adherence to ethical standards, ensuring that your content maintains the highest standards of accuracy and credibility.

12. Feedback and Learning:

Foster a culture of feedback and continuous learning. Encourage your team to review their work, analyze audience feedback, and participate in industry training to stay current.

Building a multimedia newsroom is an ongoing process that evolves alongside the industry. By creating an environment that promotes collaboration, innovation, and skill development, you'll be well-prepared to produce multimedia journalism that resonates with your audience and stands out in the digital landscape.

Chapter 3: Reporting Techniques in Multimedia Journalism

This chapter delves into the core reporting techniques and practices that empower multimedia journalists to gather information, conduct interviews, and research stories effectively. We begin with an exploration of gathering information across various platforms.

Section 3.1: Gathering Information Across Platforms

In the digital age, information is scattered across a multitude of platforms, from traditional sources to social media and user-generated content. Multimedia journalists must navigate this diverse landscape to collect accurate and comprehensive data for their stories. This section offers insights into effective information gathering techniques:

1. Traditional Sources:

Interviews: Conduct in-depth interviews with experts, eyewitnesses, and key stakeholders to gather firsthand information and perspectives.

Official Documents: Access government reports, legal documents, and public records to support your investigative journalism.

2. Digital Platforms:

Social Media: Monitor social media platforms for breaking news, eyewitness accounts, and trends related to your story. Verify the authenticity of user-generated content.

Online Forums and Communities: Explore online forums and community platforms relevant to your topic. These spaces often contain valuable insights and discussions.

Data Mining and Analysis: Utilize data scraping tools and analysis techniques to extract information from websites, datasets, and online repositories.

3. Multimedia Content:

Visual Content: Analyze and utilize multimedia content, such as images and videos, to supplement your reporting. Ensure proper attribution and permissions.

Audio Recordings: Incorporate audio recordings from interviews or events to provide context and authenticity in your stories.

4. Cross-Verification:

Fact-Checking: Rigorously fact-check information from multiple sources to ensure accuracy and credibility.

Multiple Perspectives: Seek diverse perspectives and viewpoints to present a balanced and comprehensive narrative.

5. Ethical Considerations:

Privacy and Consent: Respect the privacy and obtain the consent of individuals you interview or feature in your multimedia journalism.

Sensitivity: Approach sensitive topics with empathy and sensitivity, considering the potential impact on subjects and audiences.

6. Organization and Documentation:

Digital Tools: Utilize digital note-taking and organization tools to manage and categorize gathered information efficiently.

Attribution: Keep meticulous records of your sources, including URLs, publication dates, and contact information for potential follow-up.

Effective information gathering is the foundation of quality journalism. In the digital landscape, multimedia journalists must harness a wide range of sources, platforms, and techniques to assemble a complete and accurate picture of their stories. This section provides the initial building blocks for your reporting journey, which we will continue to expand upon in the following sections of this chapter.

Section 3.2: Conducting Interviews for Multimedia

Interviews are a cornerstone of multimedia journalism, allowing journalists to gather insights, quotes, and personal experiences that breathe life into their stories. In this section, we will explore the art of conducting interviews tailored for multimedia storytelling:

1. Preparing for the Interview:

Research: Thoroughly research your interviewee and the topic at hand. Understanding their background and perspective will help you ask informed questions.

Equipment Check: Ensure that your recording equipment, whether it's a microphone, smartphone, or camera, is in working order and properly set up.

2. Choosing the Right Format:

In-Person Interviews: Face-to-face interviews can foster rapport and allow you to capture visual elements, such as body language and facial expressions.

Phone or Online Interviews: These are useful for reaching interviewees in distant locations or for time-sensitive stories. Make sure you have a clear audio connection.

3. Framing Your Questions:

Open-Ended Questions: Encourage interviewees to provide detailed responses by asking open-ended questions that begin with "what," "how," "why," or "tell me about."

Follow-Up Questions: Be prepared to ask follow-up questions to delve deeper into specific points or to seek clarification.

4. Active Listening:

Engage Actively: Listen attentively to your interviewee's responses, and be ready to adjust your questions based on their answers.

Body Language: Maintain eye contact and open body language to show you are engaged and interested.

5. Visual and Audio Considerations:

Framing and Composition: If you're conducting a video interview, pay attention to framing and composition to ensure a visually appealing result.

Microphone Placement: Position microphones for clear audio capture and minimize background noise.

6. Building Rapport:

Establish Trust: Make interviewees feel comfortable and respected. Building rapport often leads to more candid and insightful responses.

Empathy: Show empathy, especially when discussing sensitive or emotional topics. Be respectful of personal boundaries.

7. Ethics and Consent:

Informed Consent: Clearly explain the purpose of the interview, how the information will be used, and obtain informed consent for recording and use of the interview.

Privacy: Respect an interviewee's request for anonymity or confidentiality if applicable.

8. Backup and Redundancy:

Backup Recordings: Always have a backup recording method in case of equipment failure or technical issues.

9. Post-Interview:

Transcription: Transcribe the interview for reference and to aid in accurate quoting.

Follow-Up: If necessary, follow up with interviewees for clarification or additional information.

Conducting effective interviews is an art that requires practice and skill development. Whether you're gathering audio, video, or written content, the ability to draw out meaningful insights from your sources is essential for creating engaging and informative multimedia journalism. This section provides you with the fundamentals to conduct interviews that enrich your stories and captivate your audience.

Section 3.3: Fact-Checking and Ethical Considerations

In the realm of multimedia journalism, accuracy and ethical integrity are paramount. This section explores the crucial steps of fact-checking and ethical considerations that must guide your reporting process:

1. Fact-Checking:

Verify Sources: Cross-reference information from multiple credible sources to confirm accuracy. Avoid relying solely on a single source, especially unverified social media content.

Confirm Dates and Details: Ensure that dates, names, and specific details are correct. Small errors can erode trust in your reporting.

Check Visual Content: Scrutinize images and videos for authenticity. Look for signs of manipulation or use of stock footage presented as current events.

Quotes and Attribution: Verify the accuracy of quotes attributed to interviewees. Review your notes and recordings to confirm the veracity of statements.

2. Ethical Guidelines:

Privacy and Consent: Respect individuals' privacy and obtain informed consent when featuring them in your multimedia stories. Consider the potential consequences of revealing sensitive information.

Accuracy and Fairness: Strive for accuracy and fairness in your reporting. Present a balanced view of the subject matter, providing multiple perspectives when appropriate.

Avoid Plagiarism: Cite your sources and provide proper attribution for quotes, images, and any borrowed content. Plagiarism undermines your credibility as a journalist.

Sensitivity: Approach stories with sensitivity, especially those involving trauma, tragedy, or vulnerable populations. Balance the public's right to know with ethical reporting.

Minimize Harm: Consider the potential harm your reporting may cause and take steps to minimize it. Use discretion when sharing graphic or distressing content.

Conflicts of Interest: Be transparent about any conflicts of interest that could affect your reporting. Maintain independence and avoid situations that compromise your integrity.

3. Editorial Review:

Editorial Oversight: Subject your work to editorial review. Editors can provide valuable feedback, fact-checking, and ensure compliance with ethical guidelines.

Corrections and Retractions: If errors are discovered after publication, promptly issue corrections and retractions. Transparency in addressing mistakes is crucial for maintaining trust.

4. Digital Verification:

Digital Forensics: Utilize digital verification techniques to assess the authenticity of online content, including images and videos. Tools like reverse image searches and metadata analysis can be invaluable.

5. Continuous Learning:

Stay Informed: Stay updated on evolving ethical standards and practices in journalism. Participate in training and workshops to enhance your ethical reporting skills.

6. Ethical Dilemmas:

Ethical Consultation: Seek guidance from colleagues or ethics experts when faced with complex ethical dilemmas. Discussing such situations can lead to more ethical decision-making.

Maintaining the highest ethical standards is not only a moral imperative but also essential for the credibility and trustworthiness of multimedia journalism. By rigorously fact-checking your content and adhering to ethical guidelines, you uphold the integrity of your work and contribute to the responsible dissemination of information to your audience.

Chapter 4: Writing for Multimedia

This chapter delves into the art of crafting multimedia news stories that engage and inform audiences across various platforms. We commence with Section 4.1, which explores the fundamental aspects of structuring multimedia news stories:

Section 4.1: Structuring Multimedia News Stories

Effective storytelling is the cornerstone of multimedia journalism. Structuring your news stories appropriately ensures that your audience can easily navigate and understand the information you're presenting. In this section, we'll explore key considerations for structuring multimedia news stories:

1. The Inverted Pyramid:

Begin with the most critical information at the top of your story, followed by supporting details in descending order of importance. This structure allows readers to grasp the main points quickly.

2. Multimedia Elements:

Determine which multimedia elements (images, videos, audio clips, infographics) will enhance your story. Place these elements strategically within the narrative to provide context and visual engagement.

3. Headlines and Subheadings:

Craft clear, attention-grabbing headlines that convey the essence of your story. Use subheadings to break down the story into sections, making it easier for readers to scan and find relevant information.

4. Lead and Hook:

Your lead (or lede) should encapsulate the most crucial aspects of the story and entice readers to continue. A compelling hook at the beginning can draw readers into the narrative.

5. Multimedia Integration:

Seamlessly integrate multimedia elements into your text. For instance, describe the significance of an image or video within the story.

6. Hyperlinks and References:

Include hyperlinks to relevant sources, background information, or related articles. Ensure that these links enhance the reader's understanding without interrupting the flow.

7. Clear Attribution:

Clearly attribute quotes, data, and multimedia elements to their sources. Provide context for how and why this information is relevant to the story.

8. Story Flow:

Maintain a logical flow in your narrative. Ensure that each section or paragraph naturally transitions to the next, creating a coherent and engaging reading experience.

9. Multimedia Captions:

Write informative captions for multimedia elements, explaining their relevance and providing any necessary context. Captions should complement the text rather than repeat it.

10. Audience Engagement:

Encourage audience engagement through interactive elements such as polls, surveys, or user-generated content. Invite readers to participate and share their perspectives.

11. Mobile Optimization:

As mobile devices are a significant platform for news consumption, ensure that your story is optimized for mobile viewing. Use responsive design to adapt to various screen sizes.

12. Accessibility:

Consider accessibility for all readers, including those with disabilities. Provide alternative text for images, closed captions for videos, and ensure the text is easily readable.

13. Multimedia Transitions:

Use transitions between multimedia elements and text to guide readers smoothly through the story. Ensure that transitions feel natural and add to the narrative.

Structured storytelling is a powerful tool in multimedia journalism. By organizing your news stories effectively, you not only enhance reader comprehension but also create an engaging and immersive experience. In subsequent sections of this chapter, we will delve deeper into writing techniques, styles, and best practices for multimedia journalism.

Section 4.2: Crafting Engaging Headlines and Leads

The headline and lead of your multimedia news story serve as the gateway to capturing your audience's attention. In this section, we will explore the art of crafting headlines and leads that entice readers and encourage them to delve deeper into your story:

1. The Headline:

Concise Clarity: A headline should be clear and concise, summarizing the main point of the story in a few words. Avoid jargon or overly complex language.

Relevance: Ensure that your headline accurately reflects the content of the story. Misleading headlines can erode trust with your audience.

Engagement: Craft headlines that pique curiosity or emotion. Questions, strong verbs, and intriguing statements can draw readers in.

Keyword Optimization: Consider relevant keywords for search engine optimization (SEO) while keeping the headline readable and engaging.

2. The Lead:

Hook the Reader: The lead should immediately engage the reader. Start with a compelling anecdote, a surprising fact, or a thought-provoking question.

Conciseness: Keep the lead succinct while conveying the most critical information. The goal is to capture attention, not provide an exhaustive explanation.

The Five Ws and H: Address the essential questions of who, what, when, where, why, and how in the lead to provide context.

Inverted Pyramid: While the lead should be engaging, remember the inverted pyramid structure, placing the most crucial information first.

Multimedia Integration: If multimedia elements are central to your story, consider starting with a multimedia lead, such as an impactful image or video clip.

3. Audience-Centered Approach:

Know Your Audience: Understand your target audience's interests, needs, and preferences. Tailor headlines and leads to resonate with them.

A/B Testing: Experiment with different headline and lead styles to see which resonates best with your audience. A/B testing can provide valuable insights.

4. Multimodal Headlines and Leads:

Multimedia Integration: For multimedia stories, ensure that the headline and lead effectively convey the story's multimedia elements, setting the stage for a multimedia experience.

5. SEO Considerations:

Keywords: Incorporate relevant keywords into your headline and lead while maintaining readability. This can improve your story's discoverability in online searches.

6. Ethical Considerations:

Accuracy: Ensure that your headline and lead accurately represent the story's content. Avoid sensationalism or clickbait tactics.

Sensitivity: Exercise sensitivity when crafting headlines and leads for stories involving tragedy or sensitive subjects. Balance the need for engagement with ethical reporting.

7. Consistency:**

Maintain consistency in the tone, style, and messaging between the headline, lead, and the rest of the story. Readers should feel a seamless transition from the headline to the story.

8. Editorial Review:

Have an editor or colleague review your headlines and leads. A fresh perspective can help identify areas for improvement.

Effective headlines and leads are the initial touchpoints with your audience, influencing whether readers choose to delve deeper into your multimedia story. By mastering the art of crafting engaging and informative headlines and leads, you can captivate your audience and convey the essence of your story effectively.

Section 4.3: Writing for Different Platforms

Multimedia journalism thrives in a diverse landscape of platforms, from traditional news websites to social media, podcasts, and interactive presentations. In this section, we'll explore the nuances of tailoring your writing to suit various platforms effectively:

1. Web Articles:

Concise and Scannable: Web articles should be concise, with short paragraphs and subheadings. Readers often scan web content, so make key points easily accessible.

Hyperlinks: Incorporate hyperlinks to related articles or sources, providing readers with additional context and resources.

Multimedia Integration: Embed images, videos, and other multimedia elements directly into the article to enhance engagement.

2. Social Media Posts:

Brevity: Social media posts are character-limited, so be concise. Craft punchy headlines and use relevant hashtags to increase discoverability.

Visual Appeal: Pair posts with compelling images or videos to grab attention. Ensure that your content is mobile-friendly.

Engagement: Encourage likes, shares, and comments by posing questions or inviting readers to participate in discussions.

3. Podcast Scripts:

Conversational Tone: Podcasts are audio-centric, so adopt a conversational tone in your script. Use natural language and engage with your audience as if you're having a conversation.

Structured Segments: Organize your podcast script into structured segments or chapters to guide the listener through the content.

Emphasis on Audio: Highlight the importance of audio elements, such as sound effects or musical cues, within your script.

4. Video Scripts:

Visual Storytelling: Video scripts should focus on visual storytelling. Describe scenes, camera angles, and any necessary on-screen text or graphics.

Engaging Openings: Grab viewers' attention within the first few seconds. Use visuals and concise narration to set the stage.

Clear Narration: Ensure that your narration is clear, concise, and well-paced. Avoid jargon or complex language.

5. Interactive Presentations:

Structured Navigation: Create an interactive presentation with clear navigation paths. Ensure that readers can easily explore different sections.

Multimedia Integration: Use interactive elements, such as clickable maps or data visualizations, to enhance the user experience.

Engagement Metrics: Consider incorporating interactive quizzes or surveys to engage readers and collect feedback.

6. Mobile-First Writing:

Mobile Optimization: As a general rule, ensure that your writing is mobile-friendly. Many readers access content on smartphones, so prioritize readability on smaller screens.

7. Tailored Voice and Style:

Platform Voice: Adapt your writing style and voice to the platform. Social media may allow for a more informal tone, while traditional news websites often require a more formal approach.

8. Cross-Promotion:

Link to Other Platforms: Promote content across different platforms. If you have a written article, share snippets or summaries on social media with links back to the full article.

9. SEO Optimization:

Keywords: Consider SEO when writing for web articles and social media. Incorporate relevant keywords to improve discoverability in search engines.

10. Analytics and Feedback:

Analyze Engagement: Use analytics tools to monitor how readers and viewers engage with your content on different platforms. Adapt your approach based on performance data.

Writing for different platforms requires versatility and an understanding of the unique characteristics and preferences of each medium. By tailoring your writing style, structure, and content to suit the platform, you can effectively convey your multimedia stories to diverse audiences.

Chapter 5: Visual Storytelling

In this chapter, we dive into the power of visual storytelling, a cornerstone of multimedia journalism. Section 5.1 explores the role of photography in journalism, highlighting its significance in conveying stories and information:

Section 5.1: Photography in Journalism

Photography is a universal language that transcends barriers, making it an indispensable tool in journalism. This section delves into the crucial aspects of photography in journalism:

1. Visual Impact:

Emotional Connection: Photographs have the power to evoke emotions and connect readers to the story on a personal level.

Immediate Engagement: A well-composed image can capture a reader's attention instantly, often before they even begin reading the accompanying text.

2. Storytelling Through Images:

The Decisive Moment: Henri Cartier-Bresson coined the term "decisive moment," referring to capturing an image that tells a story in a single frame.

Composition: Consider the rule of thirds, leading lines, and framing to create visually compelling compositions.

3. Photojournalism Ethics:

Accuracy and Truth: Photojournalists must maintain the highest ethical standards, ensuring that their images accurately represent the events they document.

Informed Consent: When photographing people, especially in sensitive situations, obtain informed consent whenever possible, and respect their dignity and privacy.

4. Multimedia Integration:

Enhancing Stories: Use photographs to enhance the storytelling in multimedia journalism. A series of images can create a visual narrative within the broader story.

Captions: Write informative captions that provide context, describe the scene, and identify key individuals. Captions are an integral part of photojournalism.

5. The Impact of Technology:

Smartphone Photography: Smartphone cameras have become powerful tools for journalists, enabling rapid image capture and sharing.

Editing Software: Familiarize yourself with photo editing software to enhance and adjust images while maintaining accuracy.

6. Diversity and Inclusion:

Representation: Ensure that your photography reflects the diversity of the subjects and stories you cover. Avoid stereotypes and biases in image selection.

7. Visual Story Planning:

Storyboarding: For multimedia projects, consider storyboarding to plan the visual elements of your story in advance.

Consistency: Maintain a consistent visual style throughout a multimedia project for a cohesive narrative.

8. Ethics in Image Selection:

Avoid Sensationalism: Do not use graphic or disturbing images for shock value. Consider the potential impact on your audience.

Verification: Verify the authenticity of images and their sources. Avoid using images that are misleading or misrepresentative.

Photography in journalism is a potent storytelling tool, capable of conveying complex narratives and emotions in a single frame. By understanding its power, adhering to ethical standards, and effectively integrating photographs into your multimedia storytelling, you can engage readers and amplify the impact of your journalism.

Section 5.2: Infographics and Data Visualization

Infographics and data visualization are powerful tools for conveying complex information in a visually engaging manner. In this section, we explore their role in multimedia journalism and how they can enhance the presentation of data-driven stories:

1. Visualizing Data:

Complex Data Simplified: Infographics and data visualizations simplify intricate data sets, making them accessible and understandable to a broad audience.

Storytelling with Data: Use visual elements to tell a story within the data, highlighting trends, comparisons, and key insights.

2. Types of Infographics:

Charts and Graphs: Line charts, bar graphs, and pie charts are effective for representing numerical data.

Maps: Maps and geospatial visualizations can convey location-based information and trends.

Flowcharts: Use flowcharts to illustrate processes and decision trees.

Infographic Combos: Combine different types of infographics to present a comprehensive picture of your data.

3. Design Principles:

Clarity: Keep the design clean and uncluttered, focusing on the most important data points.

Color and Typography: Use color and typography effectively to guide the viewer's attention and convey meaning.

Consistency: Maintain a consistent design style throughout the infographic for visual coherence.

4. Data Integrity:

Data Accuracy: Ensure the accuracy of data used in infographics. Misleading or erroneous data can damage credibility.

Source Attribution: Clearly attribute the sources of data used in your infographics to maintain transparency.

5. Story Integration:

Narrative Support: Infographics should support the narrative of your story. Use them to reinforce key points or provide context.

Responsive Design: Ensure that infographics are responsive and display well on various devices, including mobile phones and tablets.

6. User Interaction:

Interactive Infographics: Consider creating interactive infographics that allow users to explore data further by hovering over or clicking on elements.

Engagement: Interactive elements can enhance user engagement and encourage exploration of the data.

7. Ethical Considerations:

Avoid Misrepresentation: Ensure that your infographics accurately represent the data and avoid distorting information for dramatic effect.

Privacy: When visualizing data involving individuals, respect their privacy rights and anonymize the data when necessary.

8. Tools and Software:

Design Software: Familiarize yourself with graphic design software like Adobe Illustrator, as well as data visualization tools such as Tableau or Datawrapper.

Online Platforms: Explore online platforms and templates that facilitate infographic creation, even for those without extensive design skills.

9. Accessibility:

Alt Text: Provide alternative text for images and charts within infographics to make them accessible to individuals with visual impairments.

Infographics and data visualizations are potent storytelling tools in multimedia journalism, allowing you to convey complex information in an engaging and easily digestible format. By mastering the design principles and ethical considerations associated with visualizing data, you can create compelling visuals that enhance the impact of your multimedia stories.

Section 5.3: Incorporating Video into Stories

Video is a dynamic and immersive medium that can enrich multimedia journalism by providing viewers with a visual and auditory experience. In this section, we explore the integration of video into storytelling and its significance in multimedia journalism:

1. Visual Impact:

Engaging Visuals: Video offers a powerful way to engage your audience by combining moving images, sound, and storytelling.

Emotional Connection: The combination of visuals and sound can evoke emotions and immerse viewers in the story.

2. Types of Video Content:

News Packages: Traditional news packages combine footage, interviews, and narration to provide comprehensive coverage of a story.

Interviews and Profiles: Create video interviews or profiles of key figures in your story to add a personal touch.

Live Reporting: Live video reporting allows for real-time coverage of events, offering immediacy and authenticity.

Documentaries: Longer-form video storytelling can delve into in-depth reporting and investigative journalism.

3. Production Considerations:

Planning: Plan your video content carefully, outlining the story structure, shots, and interviews needed.

Equipment: Invest in quality video recording equipment, including cameras, microphones, and lighting, to ensure professional production.

Editing: Video editing software is essential for assembling footage, adding narration or voiceovers, and refining the final product.

4. Story Integration:

Narrative Alignment: Ensure that video content aligns with the narrative of your story. Videos should enhance the text rather than duplicate it.

Transitions: Use transitions between video clips and text to maintain a smooth and coherent storytelling flow.

5. Accessibility:

Closed Captions: Include closed captions in your videos to make them accessible to individuals with hearing impairments.

Visual Descriptions: Provide visual descriptions or audio descriptions for scenes or visuals in your videos for those with visual impairments.

6. Ethical Considerations:

Authenticity: Ensure that video content accurately represents events or interviews. Avoid manipulative editing or staging.

Privacy: Respect individuals' privacy when filming in public or private spaces. Obtain consent when necessary.

7. Engagement and Interaction:

Interactive Videos: Create interactive elements within videos, such as clickable links or embedded quizzes, to engage viewers.

Social Sharing: Encourage viewers to share videos on social media platforms to extend their reach.

8. Mobile Optimization:

Responsive Design: Optimize video content for mobile viewing, as a significant portion of viewers access videos on smartphones and tablets.

9. Hosting Platforms:

YouTube: YouTube is a popular platform for hosting and sharing videos. Consider using it to reach a broader audience.

Video Embedding: Embed videos in your online articles or multimedia presentations to create a seamless viewing experience.

10. Analytics:

Viewership Data: Use analytics tools to track viewership and engagement with your video content. This data can inform future video production.

Video is a dynamic storytelling medium that can enhance the impact of multimedia journalism by offering viewers a rich and immersive experience. By understanding video production, ethical considerations, and strategies for engagement, you can effectively incorporate video into your multimedia stories and captivate your audience.

Chapter 6: Audio Reporting and Podcasting

This chapter delves into the realm of audio reporting and podcasting, which offer unique opportunities for storytelling through sound. In Section 6.1, we explore podcasting as a journalism medium and its significance in the multimedia landscape:

Section 6.1: Podcasting as a Journalism Medium

Podcasting has emerged as a dynamic medium for journalism, allowing for in-depth storytelling and engaging with audiences through audio. This section delves into the role of podcasting in journalism:

1. The Power of Audio:

Emotional Connection: Audio storytelling has a unique ability to create emotional connections with listeners through the power of voice and sound.

Accessibility: Podcasts are easily accessible to a wide audience, providing flexibility for when and where listeners can engage with the content.

2. Types of Podcasts:

News and Current Affairs: Podcasts can cover breaking news, investigative journalism, and in-depth analysis of current events.

Narrative Storytelling: Create narrative-driven podcasts that take listeners on a journey, exploring diverse topics and experiences.

Interviews and Conversations: Podcasts often feature interviews with experts, newsmakers, or individuals with unique perspectives.

3. Production Considerations:

Content Planning: Carefully plan the content, structure, and episodes of your podcast series to maintain a coherent narrative.

Recording Quality: Invest in quality microphones and sound recording equipment to ensure clear and professional audio.

Editing: Use audio editing software to refine recordings, remove background noise, and add music or sound effects when appropriate.

4. Story Integration:

Complementary Content: Podcasts can complement written articles or multimedia presentations, offering an additional layer of storytelling.

Transcripts: Provide transcripts for your podcasts to make them accessible to individuals with hearing impairments and for reference.

5. Distribution and Platforms:

Podcast Hosting: Use podcast hosting platforms to publish and distribute your episodes. Popular platforms include Apple Podcasts, Spotify, and Google Podcasts.

Website Integration: Embed podcast episodes on your website or multimedia presentations to offer a seamless user experience.

6. Engagement and Interaction:

Audience Interaction: Encourage listener engagement through social media, listener feedback, or Q&A segments in your podcast.

Reviews and Ratings: Encourage listeners to leave reviews and ratings on podcast platforms to increase discoverability.

7. Ethics and Accuracy:

Fact-Checking: Maintain the same rigorous fact-checking standards for your podcasts as you would for written articles or video content.

Transparency: Be transparent about your sources, methodology, and any potential conflicts of interest.

8. Promotion and Monetization:

Promotional Strategies: Promote your podcast through social media, newsletters, and collaborations with other podcasts or media outlets.

Monetization: Explore monetization options, such as sponsorships, advertisements, or crowdfunding, to sustain your podcasting efforts.

9. Analytics:

Listener Insights: Use podcast analytics to gain insights into listener demographics, behavior, and engagement to refine your content.

Podcasting is a versatile and engaging medium for journalism, offering a unique way to connect with audiences through the power of audio. By understanding podcast production, ethical considerations, and strategies for promotion and engagement, you can harness the potential of podcasting to tell compelling multimedia stories.

Section 6.2: Recording and Editing Audio

Effective audio reporting and podcasting rely on high-quality recordings and skillful editing. In this section, we explore the essential techniques and tools for recording and editing audio in journalism:

1. Recording Equipment:

Microphones: Invest in a quality microphone suited for your recording needs. Dynamic microphones are ideal for interviews, while condenser microphones are excellent for studio settings.

Audio Recorders: Use portable audio recorders for field reporting. Select models with features like adjustable gain and multiple input options.

Smartphones: Modern smartphones have built-in microphones suitable for recording interviews and ambient sounds. There are also smartphone apps designed for high-quality audio recording.

2. Location Considerations:

Background Noise: Choose quiet locations for recording to minimize background noise. Use windshields or pop filters to reduce unwanted sounds.

Acoustics: Consider the room's acoustics. Soft furnishings and materials can help dampen echoes and improve sound quality.

3. Interview Techniques:

Microphone Placement: Position microphones close to the speaker's mouth for clear audio. Use lavalier microphones for hands-free recording during interviews.

Recording Levels: Monitor and adjust recording levels to prevent distortion or clipping. Test audio levels before important interviews.

Preparation: Prepare interviewees by explaining the process and ensuring they speak clearly and at a consistent pace.

4. Scripting and Narration:

Scripting: Write scripts for narration or scripted segments. Practice reading scripts to ensure a natural and engaging delivery.

Voice Control: Use vocal techniques like pacing, tone variation, and emphasis to convey information effectively.

5. Audio Editing Software:

Digital Audio Workstations (DAWs): Choose audio editing software such as Adobe Audition, Audacity, or GarageBand for editing and enhancing audio recordings.

Editing Tools: Familiarize yourself with basic editing tools like cut, copy, paste, and fade in/out for precise audio editing.

6. Editing Techniques:

Removing Noise: Use noise reduction tools to eliminate background noise or hums from recordings.

Clipping Removal: Address clipping issues by reducing audio levels in affected areas.

Enhancement: Apply equalization (EQ) to balance audio frequencies and compression to even out volume levels.

7. Transcriptions:

Transcribe Interviews: Transcribing interviews aids in editing and creating accessible content. Numerous transcription tools and services are available.

8. Exporting and Formats:

Export Formats: Export your final audio in common formats like MP3 or WAV, ensuring compatibility with podcast platforms and multimedia projects.

9. Metadata and Tagging:

Metadata: Add metadata such as episode titles, descriptions, and tags to improve discoverability on podcast platforms.

10. Quality Control:

Review: Listen to your edited audio multiple times to catch errors or inconsistencies. It's crucial to ensure high-quality content.

11. Backup: Always back up your audio recordings and edited files to prevent data loss.

Effective audio recording and editing are foundational skills for audio journalism and podcasting. By mastering the equipment, techniques, and software necessary for producing high-quality audio, you can create engaging and informative audio content for your multimedia journalism projects.

Section 6.3: Case Studies in Successful Podcasting

In this section, we examine case studies of successful podcasts in journalism, highlighting their approaches, impact, and key takeaways for aspiring podcasters and multimedia journalists:

1. "Serial" - Pioneering Long-Form Journalism:

Overview: "Serial" is often credited with popularizing narrative journalism podcasts. It explored one true crime story over multiple episodes, creating a dedicated fan base.

Key Takeaway: Long-form storytelling and serialized content can captivate audiences, provided the narrative is compelling and well-structured.

2. "The Daily" - Daily News Updates:

Overview: Produced by The New York Times, "The Daily" provides in-depth analysis of top news stories every weekday. It quickly became a trusted source for news.

Key Takeaway: Consistency and relevance are crucial for daily news podcasts. High production values and expert analysis can set a podcast apart.

3. "Radiolab" - Science and Philosophy Exploration:

Overview: "Radiolab" combines storytelling, sound design, and expert interviews to explore topics ranging from science to philosophy.

Key Takeaway: Creativity in audio storytelling and the use of soundscapes can make complex subjects accessible and engaging.

4. "Reveal" - Investigative Journalism:

Overview: "Reveal" focuses on investigative journalism, uncovering stories of injustice and corruption. It often collaborates with other news organizations.

Key Takeaway: Collaborative investigations and in-depth reporting can be translated effectively into podcast formats.

5. "Science Vs" - Fact-Based Exploration:

Overview: "Science Vs" takes on myths and controversial topics, using scientific research to debunk or confirm claims.

Key Takeaway: Combining humor, research, and a critical eye can make fact-checking engaging and informative.

6. "Criminal" - Unconventional Crime Stories:

Overview: "Criminal" explores lesser-known crime stories from around the world, often featuring interviews with those directly involved.

Key Takeaway: Unique and unconventional angles on well-trodden genres, such as crime, can attract a dedicated audience.

7. "The Moth" - Live Storytelling:

Overview: "The Moth" features real people sharing personal stories, often recorded live at events.

Key Takeaway: Authenticity and personal narratives can create a strong emotional connection with listeners.

8. "The Joe Rogan Experience" - Long-Form Conversations:

Overview: Joe Rogan's podcast features long-form conversations with a wide range of guests, from celebrities to experts in various fields.

Key Takeaway: Long-form content allows for deep dives into topics and can appeal to a broad audience.

9. "StartUp" - Behind-the-Scenes Journalism:

Overview: "StartUp" documented the creation of a podcasting company, offering a behind-the-scenes look at journalism.

Key Takeaway: Transparency and a unique premise can draw listeners into the journalistic process.

10. "The Ezra Klein Show" - In-Depth Interviews:

Overview: Ezra Klein's podcast features in-depth interviews with thought leaders and experts on a wide range of topics.

Key Takeaway: Thoughtful and well-researched interviews can provide valuable insights and attract an intellectually curious audience.

These case studies demonstrate the diverse approaches and formats that successful podcasts in journalism can take. Whether through long-form storytelling, investigative reporting, or thought-provoking interviews, podcasting offers a platform for innovative and impactful journalism in the multimedia landscape.

Chapter 7: The Role of Social Media

In Chapter 7, we explore the integral role of social media in contemporary journalism. Section 7.1 focuses on how journalists can effectively leverage social media for the dissemination of news:

Section 7.1: Leveraging Social Media for News Dissemination

Social media platforms have become powerful tools for journalists to share news stories and engage with audiences. In this section, we delve into strategies for utilizing social media effectively in journalism:

1. Real-Time Updates:

Breaking News: Social media allows journalists to provide real-time updates on breaking news, keeping audiences informed as events unfold.

Live Reporting: Platforms like Twitter and Facebook Live enable live video reporting from the field, offering an immersive experience.

2. Audience Engagement:

Two-Way Communication: Engage with your audience through comments, messages, and interactive posts. Encourage questions and feedback.

Audience-Generated Content: User-generated content, such as eyewitness photos and videos, can complement news coverage.

3. Multimedia Storytelling:

Visual Content: Share images, videos, and infographics to make your stories more engaging and shareable.

Stories and Reels: Utilize features like Instagram Stories and Facebook Reels for short, visually appealing updates.

4. Verification and Fact-Checking:

Verify Sources: Be cautious when sharing unverified information. Use social media to verify sources and confirm facts.

Debunk Misinformation: Actively debunk false information and provide credible sources to counter misinformation.

5. Branding and Trust:

Maintain Credibility: Uphold journalistic standards on social media to build trust with your audience.

Personal Brand: Develop a professional yet approachable personal brand as a journalist, which can enhance your credibility.

6. Cross-Promotion:

Platform Integration: Promote your stories across different social media platforms to reach diverse audiences.

Hashtags: Use relevant and trending hashtags to increase the discoverability of your content.

7. Ethical Considerations:

Privacy and Consent: Respect individuals' privacy and obtain consent when sharing their images or information on social media.

Sensitivity: Exercise sensitivity when covering sensitive topics, tragedies, or emergencies on social media.

8. Data and Analytics:

Analytics Tools: Use analytics provided by social media platforms to track engagement and audience demographics, informing your content strategy.

9. Social Media Guidelines:

Newsroom Policies: Develop clear social media guidelines for your newsroom to ensure consistent and responsible use of social media.

10. Crisis Communication:

Crisis Management: Be prepared to handle crises or controversies on social media professionally and transparently.

Social media has revolutionized the way news is disseminated and consumed. By harnessing the power of social media effectively, journalists can reach wider audiences, engage with readers, and maintain credibility in the ever-evolving digital landscape.

Section 7.2: Social Media Ethics and Pitfalls

While social media offers valuable opportunities for journalism, it also presents ethical challenges and potential pitfalls. In this section, we explore the ethical considerations journalists must navigate when using social media and how to avoid common pitfalls:

1. Accuracy and Verification:

Ethical Challenge: The speed of social media can tempt journalists to prioritize speed over accuracy. Sharing unverified information can harm your credibility and misinform the public.

Solution: Uphold rigorous verification standards on social media. Confirm information with reliable sources before sharing. Clearly label unverified content as such.

2. Privacy and Consent:

Ethical Challenge: Posting sensitive or private information about individuals without their consent violates their privacy rights and ethical standards.

Solution: Obtain explicit consent when sharing personal stories or images. Respect individuals' privacy, especially in sensitive situations.

3. Sensationalism and Clickbait:

Ethical Challenge: Crafting sensational or misleading headlines and content to boost engagement can damage your credibility and deceive the audience.

Solution: Prioritize factual, informative, and responsible content. Avoid sensational language and clickbait tactics.

4. Trolling and Harassment:

Ethical Challenge: Engaging in online harassment or encouraging it through your social media presence is unethical and can harm individuals and communities.

Solution: Maintain a respectful and constructive online presence. Report and block trolls and harassment promptly.

5. Bias and Objectivity:

Ethical Challenge: Expressing personal biases or opinions on social media can compromise your objectivity as a journalist.

Solution: Maintain a professional and impartial tone on social media. Clearly distinguish between personal and professional accounts, if necessary.

6. Plagiarism and Attribution:

Ethical Challenge: Failing to attribute content properly or plagiarizing from social media sources undermines journalistic integrity.

Solution: Always credit the original source when sharing content. Cite and link to sources accurately.

7. Engagement with Sources:

Ethical Challenge: Interacting with sources or subjects of your reporting on social media can blur the lines between journalist and participant.

Solution: Maintain professionalism in your interactions with sources. Avoid taking sides or engaging in personal disputes.

8. Ethical Guidelines:

Ethical Framework: Familiarize yourself with your newsroom's or organization's social media ethics guidelines. Adhere to industry codes of ethics.

9. Transparency:

Ethical Principle: Transparency is key to building trust. Be transparent about your identity as a journalist and any potential conflicts of interest.

10. Responsibility as a Gatekeeper:

Ethical Role: Recognize your role as a gatekeeper of information. Exercise caution and responsibility in what you choose to amplify on social media.

Navigating the ethical landscape of social media is essential for journalists to maintain credibility and uphold their ethical obligations to inform the public accurately and responsibly. By adhering to ethical guidelines and being mindful of potential pitfalls, journalists can leverage social media effectively while maintaining their professional integrity.

Section 7.3: Building a Personal Brand as a Journalist

In the digital age, journalists have the opportunity to cultivate a personal brand that enhances their professional reputation and widens their reach. This section explores the importance of building a personal brand as a journalist and offers strategies for doing so effectively:

1. Why Personal Branding Matters:

Visibility: A strong personal brand increases your visibility as a journalist, making you more recognizable and memorable to your audience.

Trust and Credibility: A well-crafted personal brand can enhance your trustworthiness and credibility in the eyes of your audience.

Audience Engagement: Personal branding allows you to connect with your audience on a more personal level, fostering engagement and loyalty.

2. Define Your Niche and Voice:

Identify Your Focus: Determine the specific topics or areas of journalism that you want to be known for. Specialization can make you an authority in your niche.

Voice and Style: Develop a unique voice and writing style that sets you apart. Your tone should be consistent with your chosen niche and audience.

3. Professionalism and Consistency:

Consistent Image: Maintain a professional and consistent image across all your online profiles and content.

Profile Bios: Craft compelling and informative bios on social media profiles that reflect your expertise and interests.

4. Content Creation and Sharing:

High-Quality Content: Create and share high-quality journalism content that aligns with your brand. Regularly update your portfolio or website.

Multimedia Presence: Use various formats, including articles, videos, podcasts, and infographics, to diversify your content and reach a broader audience.

5. Engagement and Interaction:

Audience Engagement: Actively engage with your audience through comments, messages, and responses. Foster meaningful conversations around your content.

Collaborations: Collaborate with other journalists, experts, or influencers in your field to expand your network and reach.

6. Thought Leadership:

Opinion Pieces: Share well-reasoned opinion pieces and analysis to establish yourself as a thought leader in your niche.

Educational Content: Offer educational content that provides value to your audience, such as explainer articles or tutorials.

7. Use Social Media Strategically:

Platform Selection: Choose social media platforms that align with your brand and where your target audience is active.

Content Scheduling: Develop a content schedule to maintain a consistent online presence.

8. Network Building:

Networking: Attend industry events, webinars, and conferences to connect with peers and stay updated on industry trends.

LinkedIn: Optimize your LinkedIn profile to showcase your professional achievements and connect with fellow professionals.

9. Continuous Learning:

Professional Development: Invest in ongoing learning and skill development to stay at the forefront of your field.

10. Monitor and Adapt:

Analytics: Use analytics tools to monitor the performance of your personal brand efforts. Adapt your strategies based on audience feedback and data.

Building a personal brand as a journalist is an ongoing process that requires dedication and authenticity. By defining your niche, consistently producing high-quality content, engaging with your audience, and strategically using social media, you can develop a personal brand that enhances your career and strengthens your impact in the world of journalism.

Chapter 8: Multimedia Journalism Ethics and Pitfalls

In Chapter 8, we explore the complex ethical landscape of multimedia journalism. Section 8.1 focuses on the ethical considerations that journalists must navigate when engaging in multimedia reporting:

Section 8.1: Ethical Considerations in Multimedia Reporting

Multimedia reporting presents unique ethical challenges due to the convergence of different media formats. In this section, we delve into the key ethical considerations for multimedia journalists:

1. Accuracy and Verification:

Ethical Challenge: The use of multiple media formats can complicate the verification process. Journalists must ensure the accuracy of all elements in a multimedia story.

Solution: Implement rigorous fact-checking and verification procedures for all media types used in a story. Clearly label unverified content.

2. Context and Fair Representation:

Ethical Challenge: Combining text, images, videos, and graphics can influence the narrative. Journalists must ensure fair and accurate representation.

Solution: Present content in context. Avoid selective editing or visual framing that distorts the truth. Provide a balanced view of the story.

3. Privacy and Consent:

Ethical Challenge: Multimedia reporting can inadvertently invade individuals' privacy, especially when using images or videos of private moments.

Solution: Obtain informed consent when using content featuring individuals in non-public settings. Respect individuals' privacy rights.

4. Sensitivity to Vulnerable Subjects:

Ethical Challenge: Multimedia reporting may involve vulnerable subjects, such as victims of trauma or marginalized communities. Sensitivity is crucial.

Solution: Exercise utmost sensitivity when covering such subjects. Seek their informed consent and consider the potential impact on them.

5. Manipulation and Enhancement:

Ethical Challenge: The temptation to enhance visuals or audio for dramatic effect can compromise the integrity of multimedia reporting.

Solution: Refrain from manipulating or enhancing media elements in a deceptive manner. Clearly label any edited or enhanced content.

6. Attribution and Plagiarism:

Ethical Challenge: Properly attributing multimedia elements to their sources is essential. Plagiarism extends beyond text to images, videos, and graphics.

Solution: Cite and credit the sources of all media elements used in your story. Avoid using copyrighted material without permission or proper attribution.

7. Respect for Cultural Sensitivities:

Ethical Challenge: Multimedia reporting may involve diverse cultures and contexts. Journalists must respect cultural sensitivities and avoid stereotypes.

Solution: Conduct thorough research to understand cultural nuances. Engage with local experts and sources to ensure accurate representation.

8. User-Generated Content:

Ethical Challenge: Incorporating user-generated content (UGC) can be risky due to potential misinformation or bias in UGC.

Solution: Verify UGC rigorously and clearly label it as such. Explain the limitations and potential biases associated with UGC.

9. Transparent Corrections:

Ethical Principle: When errors occur in multimedia reporting, correct them promptly and transparently. Acknowledge and rectify mistakes to maintain trust.

10. Editorial Independence:

Ethical Principle: Maintain editorial independence in multimedia reporting. Avoid undue influence from advertisers, sponsors, or external pressures.

Navigating the ethical considerations in multimedia reporting requires journalists to uphold the highest standards of accuracy, fairness, and sensitivity. By adhering to ethical principles and consistently applying them to all media elements, multimedia journalists can produce stories that inform and engage while preserving trust and integrity.

Section 8.2: Common Mistakes and How to Avoid Them

While multimedia journalism offers a dynamic way to tell stories, it also comes with common pitfalls that journalists should be aware of and strive to avoid. In this section, we delve into these mistakes and provide guidance on how to steer clear of them:

1. Misrepresentation Through Visuals:

Mistake: Using visuals (images, videos, infographics) that misrepresent the context or facts of a story, leading to misinterpretation.

Prevention: Verify the authenticity and context of visuals rigorously. Provide adequate captions or context to ensure viewers understand the intended message accurately.

2. Sensationalism:

Mistake: Crafting multimedia stories for shock value rather than factual reporting, which can compromise credibility.

Prevention: Prioritize factual reporting and responsible storytelling. Avoid exaggeration and sensational language in your multimedia content.

3. Lack of Ethical Attribution:

Mistake: Failing to attribute multimedia elements to their original sources or using copyrighted material without permission.

Prevention: Always credit the sources of multimedia elements, whether it's an image, video clip, or graphic. Obtain proper permissions for copyrighted material.

4. Misleading Editing:

Mistake: Editing audio or video content in a way that distorts the truth or misrepresents events.

Prevention: Edit multimedia elements transparently and avoid manipulative editing that changes the original context or meaning. Clearly label edited content.

5. Privacy Violations:

Mistake: Invading individuals' privacy by sharing images or videos taken without their consent, especially in private settings.

Prevention: Obtain informed consent when featuring individuals in non-public contexts.

Respect privacy rights, especially in sensitive situations.

6. Insufficient Fact-Checking:

Mistake: Neglecting thorough fact-checking of all media elements in a multimedia story, leading to inaccuracies.

Prevention: Implement strict fact-checking procedures for all elements, including visuals and multimedia data. Clearly label unverified content.

7. Overlooking Cultural Sensitivities:

Mistake: Failing to consider cultural nuances or sensitivities when using multimedia elements in diverse contexts.

Prevention: Conduct comprehensive research to understand cultural norms and sensitivities. Engage with local experts and sources for guidance.

8. Disregarding User-Generated Content (UGC) Risks:

Mistake: Using UGC without adequate verification, potentially incorporating misinformation or bias into multimedia reporting.

Prevention: Thoroughly vet UGC and clearly indicate its origin. Explain the limitations and potential biases associated with UGC to your audience.

9. Neglecting Transparency in Corrections:

Mistake: Failing to correct errors or inaccuracies in multimedia content transparently and promptly.

Prevention: Acknowledge and rectify mistakes openly. Clearly communicate corrections to your audience to maintain trust.

10. Editorial Independence Compromises:

Mistake: Allowing external pressures, such as advertisers or sponsors, to influence the content and editorial independence of multimedia reporting.

Prevention: Safeguard editorial independence at all costs. Clearly delineate between editorial content and advertising or sponsorship messages.

Avoiding these common mistakes in multimedia journalism requires a commitment to ethical reporting practices, thorough fact-checking, sensitivity to diverse contexts, and a dedication to transparency and responsible storytelling. By adhering to these principles, journalists can create multimedia stories that inform and engage while upholding the highest standards of journalism ethics.

Section 8.3: Balancing Speed and Accuracy in Reporting

One of the most significant challenges in multimedia journalism is striking the right balance between delivering news quickly and ensuring accuracy and credibility. In this section, we explore the complexities of this balancing act and offer strategies for achieving it effectively:

1. The Need for Speed:

Importance of Timeliness: In the fast-paced digital age, audiences expect rapid news updates, especially during breaking news events.

Competitive Landscape: Multimedia journalists often face competition from numerous sources, including citizen journalists and social media.

2. The Risk of Inaccuracy:

Ethical Imperative: Accuracy is a fundamental ethical principle in journalism. Reporting inaccurate information can harm individuals and misinform the public.

Trust and Credibility: Consistently accurate reporting builds trust with the audience, while inaccuracies can damage a journalist's reputation and the credibility of the news organization.

3. Strategies for Balancing Speed and Accuracy:

Verification First: Prioritize verification of information before publication. Confirm facts, sources, and context rigorously.

Transparency: If you must report on unverified information due to its timeliness, clearly label it as such. Explain to your audience the steps you're taking to verify.

Collaboration: Collaborate with colleagues in your newsroom or other trusted organizations to cross-check information and ensure accuracy.

Updates and Corrections: Be prepared to update and correct your multimedia content as more information becomes available. Transparently communicate any corrections to your audience.

4. Audience Expectations:

Communication: Inform your audience about your commitment to accuracy and responsible reporting. Educate them about the challenges of reporting during breaking news events.

Engagement: Encourage audience engagement in the verification process, such as crowdsourcing information, while maintaining strict editorial oversight.

5. Ethical Considerations:

Privacy and Sensitivity: Even in the rush to report, respect privacy rights and exercise sensitivity when covering traumatic events or private matters.

Ethical Guidelines: Adhere to the ethical guidelines and standards set by your news organization and the broader journalism community.

6. Learn from Mistakes:

Accountability: Accept responsibility for errors and mistakes in reporting. Use them as opportunities for improvement and learning.

Prevent Recurrence: Implement mechanisms to prevent the recurrence of similar errors in the future.

7. Technology and Tools:

Fact-Checking Tools: Utilize fact-checking tools and resources available to verify information quickly and accurately.

Editorial Workflows: Develop efficient editorial workflows that prioritize accuracy without sacrificing speed unnecessarily.

Balancing speed and accuracy in multimedia reporting is a complex task that requires journalistic integrity, transparency, and a commitment to the highest ethical standards. By implementing verification processes, maintaining transparency with the audience, and learning from past mistakes, multimedia journalists can meet the demands of timely reporting while upholding the core principles of journalism.

Chapter 9: Tips for Multimedia Success

In Chapter 9, we provide valuable tips and strategies to help multimedia journalists excel in their field. Section 9.1 focuses on the crucial aspect of time management for multimedia journalists:

Section 9.1: Time Management for Multimedia Journalists

Effective time management is essential for multimedia journalists who juggle various media formats, deadlines, and responsibilities. Here, we explore time management tips tailored to the demands of multimedia journalism:

1. Prioritize Tasks:

Assess Urgency: Start your day by identifying the most urgent tasks, such as impending deadlines or breaking news updates.

Set Clear Goals: Define your priorities and create a to-do list, ensuring that multimedia elements like video editing, image selection, and text writing are accounted for.

2. Create a Multimedia Calendar:

Content Planning: Develop a content calendar that outlines when multimedia projects are due. Include milestones for research, scripting, filming, and editing.

Editorial Calendar: Align your multimedia calendar with the editorial calendar of your newsroom to ensure coordination.

3. Streamline Workflows:

Efficient Workflows: Optimize your multimedia workflows by identifying repetitive tasks and finding ways to automate or streamline them.

Multitasking: When feasible, work on multiple elements of a story simultaneously, such as conducting interviews while gathering visuals.

4. Time Blocks:

Allocate Blocks: Divide your day into time blocks dedicated to specific tasks, like shooting video, conducting interviews, or editing text.

Avoid Overcommitting: Be realistic about how much you can accomplish in each block and avoid overcommitting to tasks.

5. Minimize Distractions:

Digital Distractions: Turn off non-essential notifications and use apps or techniques to limit distractions during work hours.

Set Boundaries: Communicate with colleagues and family about your working hours and the importance of uninterrupted time.

6. Stay Organized:

Digital Tools: Utilize digital tools like project management software, calendar apps, and note-taking apps to stay organized.

File Management: Maintain a well-organized digital file system for multimedia assets, making it easy to find what you need quickly.

7. Regular Breaks:

Scheduled Breaks: Include short breaks in your schedule to recharge. Frequent, short breaks can boost productivity.

Physical Activity: Consider incorporating physical activity into your breaks to clear your mind and reduce stress.

8. Collaborative Tools:

Collaboration Platforms: Use collaborative tools and platforms for multimedia projects, allowing team members to work together seamlessly.

Communication: Ensure effective communication with colleagues, especially when working remotely, to avoid delays or misalignment.

9. Learn to Delegate:

Team Collaboration: If you have a team, delegate tasks according to individual strengths and expertise, enabling a more efficient workflow.

Outsourcing: When appropriate, consider outsourcing certain tasks, such as video editing or graphic design, to specialists.

10. Continuous Learning:

Skill Enhancement: Invest in ongoing training and skill development to improve your efficiency in multimedia production tools and techniques.

11. Evaluation and Adaptation:

Regular Assessment: Periodically evaluate your time management strategies. Identify areas for improvement and adjust your approach accordingly.

Effective time management is a cornerstone of success in multimedia journalism. By implementing these tips, multimedia journalists can maintain productivity, meet deadlines, and produce high-quality content across various media formats while minimizing stress and burnout.

Section 9.2: Navigating a Changing Media Landscape

The media landscape is continually evolving, presenting both challenges and opportunities for multimedia journalists. In this section, we explore strategies to effectively navigate the ever-changing media environment:

1. Stay Informed:

Media Trends: Regularly consume news and media to stay updated on emerging trends, technologies, and audience preferences.

Industry Insights: Follow industry publications, attend conferences, and engage with online communities of journalists to gain insights into the evolving landscape.

2. Adapt to New Technologies:

Tech Literacy: Develop and maintain proficiency in multimedia production tools, editing software, and emerging technologies relevant to journalism.

Experimentation: Don't hesitate to experiment with new storytelling formats, such as virtual reality, augmented reality, or interactive graphics.

3. Audience-Centric Approach:

Audience Analysis: Understand your audience's demographics, preferences, and behaviors. Tailor your multimedia content to meet their needs.

Engagement Strategies: Use social media, email newsletters, and interactive elements to engage with your audience and build a loyal following.

4. Diversify Skills:

Multimedia Skills: Expand your skill set to include a wide range of multimedia formats, from podcasts and live video to data visualization and 360-degree storytelling.

Cross-Platform Proficiency: Be adaptable across different media platforms, including websites, social media, mobile apps, and emerging platforms.

5. Collaborate and Network:

Cross-Collaboration: Collaborate with colleagues from various media disciplines, such as photographers, videographers, and data journalists, to create comprehensive multimedia stories.

Networking: Build a strong professional network within the industry to stay informed about opportunities and trends.

6. Agile Storytelling:

Responsive Reporting: Be prepared to adapt quickly to developing stories, particularly in fast-moving news cycles like breaking news or crises.

Story Formats: Consider different storytelling formats, such as explainer videos, live Q&A sessions, or interactive timelines, to engage your audience effectively.

7. Data-Driven Journalism:

Data Analysis: Embrace data journalism techniques to uncover insights and trends within datasets, providing in-depth analysis to your audience.

Visualizations: Use data visualizations and infographics to make complex information accessible and engaging.

8. Ethical Considerations:

Ethical Adherence: Maintain ethical standards and principles in all your multimedia journalism efforts, considering the impact of your content on the public.

Transparency: Clearly communicate your journalistic approach and sources to your audience to build trust.

9. Continuous Learning:

Skill Development: Invest in continuous learning and professional development to stay ahead in an evolving field.

Feedback: Seek feedback from peers, mentors, and your audience to refine your multimedia journalism skills.

10. Adaptability and Resilience:

Embrace Change: Be adaptable and open to change. Embrace new challenges and opportunities as the media landscape evolves.

Resilience: Develop resilience to handle the pressures of multimedia journalism, including tight deadlines and audience feedback.

Navigating a changing media landscape requires a proactive approach, a commitment to lifelong learning, and an unwavering dedication to quality journalism. By staying informed, adapting to new technologies, and fostering a deep understanding of your audience, you can thrive in the dynamic world of multimedia journalism.

Section 9.3: Staying Updated on Multimedia Trends

To excel in multimedia journalism, it's crucial to stay informed about the latest trends and innovations shaping the industry. In this section, we explore strategies for staying updated on multimedia trends:

1. Multimedia Industry Publications:

Subscribe and Read: Regularly subscribe to and read multimedia-focused publications, both online and in print. These publications often provide in-depth insights into industry trends and emerging technologies.

Industry Reports: Pay attention to research reports and studies released by industry associations and consulting firms. These reports can offer valuable data on multimedia consumption patterns and emerging technologies.

2. Online Communities and Forums:

Join Communities: Become a member of online forums and communities dedicated to multimedia journalism. Engage in discussions, ask questions, and share your experiences with fellow multimedia professionals.

Social Media Groups: Follow social media groups and pages dedicated to multimedia journalism.

Platforms like LinkedIn, Twitter, and Facebook have active multimedia journalism communities.

3. Attend Multimedia Workshops and Conferences:

Professional Development: Participate in multimedia workshops, seminars, and conferences. These events often feature presentations by industry experts and hands-on training sessions.

Networking: Take advantage of networking opportunities at these events to connect with peers, exchange ideas, and stay updated on the latest trends.

4. Online Courses and Webinars:

E-Learning Platforms: Enroll in online courses related to multimedia journalism offered by e-learning platforms like Coursera, edX, or LinkedIn Learning.

Webinars: Attend webinars conducted by industry leaders and organizations. These webinars can provide insights into cutting-edge multimedia techniques and technologies.

5. Multimedia Journalism Awards and Competitions:

Awards Programs: Keep an eye on multimedia journalism awards programs and competitions. Studying the winning entries can offer valuable insights into innovative storytelling approaches.

Participate: Consider submitting your own multimedia projects to awards programs to gain recognition and feedback.

6. Industry Blogs and Podcasts:

Multimedia Blogs: Follow blogs and podcasts hosted by multimedia journalists and experts. These platforms often share practical tips, case studies, and discussions on current trends.

Guest Appearances: Explore opportunities to be a guest on multimedia-related podcasts or blogs to share your expertise and learn from others in the field.

7. Collaboration and Knowledge Sharing:

Collaborate with Peers: Collaborate with other multimedia journalists on projects and knowledge sharing. Peer-to-peer learning can be a rich source of trend awareness.

Professional Organizations: Join professional journalism organizations that focus on multimedia reporting. These organizations often provide resources, webinars, and networking events.

8. Experimentation and Hands-On Learning:

Hands-On Practice: Continuously experiment with multimedia tools and techniques. Hands-on experience is one of the most effective ways to stay updated.

Try New Tools: Explore and test new multimedia tools, software, and platforms as they emerge in the market. Familiarize yourself with their capabilities and potential applications.

9. Audience Feedback:

Audience Engagement: Pay attention to audience feedback on your multimedia content. Comments, shares, and discussions can reveal trends and preferences among your viewers.

Iterative Improvement: Use audience feedback to iteratively improve your multimedia storytelling and content strategies.

Staying updated on multimedia trends is an ongoing commitment that requires curiosity, a willingness to learn, and an active engagement with the multimedia journalism community. By embracing these strategies, multimedia journalists can remain at the forefront of their field, delivering compelling and relevant stories to their audiences.

Chapter 10: Case Studies in Multimedia Journalism

Chapter 10 delves into real-world examples of multimedia journalism to provide valuable insights and inspiration for multimedia journalists. Section 10.1 focuses on award-winning multimedia reporting:

Section 10.1: Award-Winning Multimedia Reporting

In this section, we explore case studies of award-winning multimedia journalism projects that have set high standards in the field. These examples showcase the innovative use of various media formats to tell compelling stories and engage audiences. Here are a few notable award-winning multimedia reporting projects:

1. "Snow Fall: The Avalanche at Tunnel Creek" (The New York Times):

Description: This Pulitzer Prize-winning multimedia feature combines text, photos, videos, and interactive graphics to tell the harrowing story of a deadly avalanche in Washington State.

Innovation: The project uses parallax scrolling and multimedia elements to immerse readers in the narrative, enhancing engagement and understanding.

2. "The Life of Syrian Refugee Children" (BBC News):

Description: This multimedia series sheds light on the lives of Syrian refugee children in Lebanon through video documentaries, photo galleries, and in-depth articles.

Impact: The project humanizes the refugee crisis and provides a comprehensive view of the challenges faced by displaced children.

3. "The Last Generation" (National Geographic):

Description: National Geographic's multimedia project explores the effects of climate change on the Marshall Islands. It includes articles, photos, videos, and interactive maps.

Engagement: The project's interactive maps and visuals allow readers to explore the impact of rising sea levels on the islands, making the issue tangible and urgent.

4. "The Panama Papers" (ICIJ):

Description: This collaborative investigative project used multimedia elements to expose the hidden wealth of the world's elite, based on leaked documents.

Impact: The project's use of interactive data visualizations and storytelling drew global attention to the issue of offshore tax havens and led to significant policy changes.

5. "A Photographic Journey of Rohingya Refugees" (Al Jazeera):

Description: This multimedia feature combines powerful photojournalism with audio narratives to provide an intimate look at the plight of Rohingya refugees.

Storytelling: The project effectively uses images and audio to convey the personal stories and struggles of the Rohingya people, fostering empathy among viewers.

6. "The Wall: A Borderline Crisis" (ProPublica and The Texas Tribune):

Description: This multimedia investigation explores the impact of the U.S.-Mexico border wall through interactive maps, videos, and in-depth reporting.

Informative: The project offers a comprehensive look at the border wall's consequences, making complex issues accessible to a wide audience.

These award-winning multimedia reporting projects demonstrate the power of combining diverse media formats to create impactful and engaging journalism. They serve as valuable examples of effective storytelling techniques and innovation in the field of multimedia journalism, inspiring journalists to push the boundaries of their craft.

Section 10.2: Successful Multimedia News Organizations

In Section 10.2, we examine multimedia news organizations that have successfully adapted to the changing media landscape and set benchmarks for multimedia journalism. These organizations have embraced various media formats to deliver news effectively and engage their audiences. Here are notable examples:

1. The New York Times:

Multimedia Excellence: The New York Times is renowned for its multimedia storytelling, including interactive graphics, videos, podcasts, and virtual reality experiences.

Innovative Projects: The publication's "The Daily" podcast and interactive features like "The 1619 Project" have garnered widespread acclaim for their innovation and impact.

2. BBC News:

Global Reach: BBC News has a strong global presence with multimedia content that covers diverse topics, regions, and formats.

Video Reporting: BBC's video documentaries and live coverage of major events are well-regarded for their depth and immediacy.

3. National Geographic:

Visual Storytelling: National Geographic excels in visual storytelling, using multimedia to transport audiences to remote locations and showcase the beauty and challenges of our world.

Science and Environment Focus: The organization's multimedia features often revolve around science, exploration, and environmental issues.

4. ProPublica:

Investigative Excellence: ProPublica is known for its in-depth investigative reporting, often presented through multimedia elements like data visualizations and interactive articles.

Collaborative Projects: ProPublica collaborates with other news organizations to amplify the impact of its investigative journalism.

5. The Guardian:

Interactive Journalism: The Guardian incorporates interactive storytelling elements into its reporting, offering readers engaging and informative multimedia experiences.

Data Journalism: The publication is recognized for its data-driven journalism, often using multimedia to convey complex information.

6. Al Jazeera:

Global Coverage: Al Jazeera provides comprehensive multimedia coverage of global events, with a particular focus on stories from the Middle East and Asia.

Human Interest Stories: The organization often features human interest stories with multimedia elements that bring personal narratives to the forefront.

7. Vox Media:

Explainer Videos: Vox Media is known for its explainer videos, which use multimedia to break down complex topics and make them accessible to a broad audience.

Podcast Network: Vox Media operates a successful podcast network, including popular shows like "Today, Explained" and "The Weeds."

8. Reuters:

Global Journalism: Reuters offers multimedia news coverage with a global reach, emphasizing video reports and multimedia packages that cover breaking news and in-depth analysis.

Data Services: Beyond journalism, Reuters provides data services and visualizations to clients worldwide.

These successful multimedia news organizations showcase the diverse approaches to multimedia journalism. They leverage various media formats, storytelling techniques, and technology to deliver news, engage audiences, and maintain relevance in the evolving media landscape. Multimedia journalists can draw inspiration from their successes to enhance their own storytelling practices and adapt to changing audience preferences.

Section 10.3: Lessons Learned from Notable Cases

In Section 10.3, we draw lessons from notable cases in multimedia journalism that can serve as valuable takeaways for aspiring journalists and news organizations. These lessons encompass a range of aspects, from storytelling techniques to ethical considerations:

1. Storytelling Innovation:

Lesson: Innovative storytelling techniques, such as parallax scrolling, interactive graphics, and immersive multimedia experiences, can captivate audiences and enhance understanding.

Example: "Snow Fall" by The New York Times demonstrated the power of parallax scrolling and multimedia integration to create an immersive narrative.

2. Audience-Centric Approach:

Lesson: Understanding your audience's preferences, demographics, and behaviors is crucial. Tailor your multimedia content to meet their needs and engage them effectively.

Example: BBC News' multimedia coverage adapts to different regions and topics, ensuring relevance and engagement for diverse audiences.

3. Data-Driven Journalism:

Lesson: Data analysis and visualization can enrich multimedia reporting, making complex information accessible and compelling.

Example: ProPublica's use of data visualizations in investigative reporting highlights the impact of data-driven journalism.

4. Collaboration and Partnerships:

Lesson: Collaborating with other news organizations, experts, and communities can amplify the reach and impact of multimedia journalism projects.

Example: The collaborative efforts in "The Panama Papers" investigation showcased the power of cross-border partnerships.

5. Ethical Considerations:

Lesson: Upholding ethical standards is non-negotiable in multimedia journalism. Transparency, fact-checking, and sensitivity are essential.

Example: "A Photographic Journey of Rohingya Refugees" by Al Jazeera demonstrated ethical storytelling by respecting the subjects' dignity and consent.

6. Global Coverage:

Lesson: Providing comprehensive global coverage through multimedia reporting ensures a broad audience reach and relevance.

Example: Al Jazeera's multimedia content spans the globe, making diverse stories accessible to a worldwide audience.

7. Interactivity and Engagement:

Lesson: Interactivity, such as comment sections, polls, and user-generated content, can foster audience engagement and facilitate a sense of community.

Example: Vox Media's explainer videos engage audiences by simplifying complex topics and inviting viewer participation.

8. Visual Storytelling:

Lesson: Visual storytelling through photos, videos, and infographics is a powerful way to convey emotions, context, and information.

Example: National Geographic's multimedia projects effectively utilize visual storytelling to transport audiences to different worlds.

9. Impactful Investigative Reporting:

Lesson: Investigative multimedia reporting can lead to significant social and political change when it exposes hidden truths and wrongdoing.

Example: The "Panama Papers" investigation resulted in policy changes and increased transparency in offshore financial practices.

10. Adaptation and Innovation:

Lesson: Successful multimedia journalism organizations continuously adapt to emerging technologies and audience preferences while fostering innovation.

Example: The Guardian's use of interactive elements and data journalism showcases a commitment to adapting to the digital age.

These lessons from notable cases in multimedia journalism offer valuable insights for journalists, news organizations, and aspiring multimedia professionals. By applying these lessons, multimedia journalists can create impactful, ethical, and engaging content that resonates with audiences in an ever-evolving media landscape.

Chapter 11: The Future of Multimedia Journalism

In Chapter 11, we explore the evolving landscape of multimedia journalism and what the future holds for the field. Section 11.1 delves into emerging technologies that are shaping the future of journalism:

Section 11.1: Emerging Technologies in Journalism

As technology continues to advance, multimedia journalism is poised to undergo significant transformations. Here, we examine some of the emerging technologies that are expected to play a pivotal role in the future of journalism:

1. Virtual Reality (VR) and Augmented Reality (AR):

Immersive Storytelling: VR and AR technologies offer immersive storytelling experiences. Journalists can use VR to transport readers to the heart of a story, while AR can overlay information on the real world.

Examples: The use of VR in reporting on conflict zones or AR for interactive educational pieces.

2. Artificial Intelligence (AI):

Automated Content Generation: AI-driven algorithms can assist in generating news articles, data analysis, and even personalized content for readers.

Fact-Checking: AI tools can aid in fact-checking and detecting misinformation in real-time.

3. 5G Connectivity:

Faster Streaming: The rollout of 5G networks will enable faster and more reliable streaming of multimedia content, including live video reporting.

Enhanced Mobile Experiences: Mobile users will enjoy seamless access to multimedia content, leading to increased mobile journalism.

4. Data Journalism and Visualization:

Data-Driven Stories: The use of big data analytics and visualization tools will continue to drive data journalism, enabling journalists to uncover hidden trends and present them visually.

Interactive Dashboards: Readers can interact with data-driven stories through dynamic and user-friendly dashboards.

5. Blockchain Technology:

Transparency and Trust: Blockchain can enhance transparency in journalism by providing secure and immutable records of content creation and distribution.

Micropayments: Blockchain-based micropayments can enable new revenue models for quality journalism.

6. Chatbots and Personalization:

Audience Engagement: Chatbots can interact with readers, answer questions, and personalize content recommendations based on user preferences.

24/7 Accessibility: Chatbots provide around-the-clock access to news and information.

7. Wearable Technology:

Reporting on the Go: Journalists equipped with wearables like smart glasses can capture and broadcast events from their perspective in real-time.

Enhanced Field Reporting: Wearable devices can enhance field reporting by offering hands-free recording and live-streaming capabilities.

8. Voice-Activated News:

Voice Assistants: News organizations are exploring voice-activated platforms like Amazon Alexa and Google Assistant to deliver news updates and interact with audiences.

Podcasting: The rise of voice-activated speakers has boosted the popularity of news podcasts.

9. 360-Degree Video and Live Streaming:

Immersive Live Reporting: Journalists can use 360-degree video and live streaming to provide audiences with immersive, real-time experiences of events.

Audience Engagement: Live Q&A sessions and audience interaction during live streams enhance engagement.

10. Ethical Considerations:

Privacy and Security: As these technologies evolve, ethical considerations around privacy, security, and responsible use become increasingly important.

The future of multimedia journalism promises to be a dynamic and technologically driven landscape. Journalists and news organizations that embrace these emerging technologies while upholding journalistic integrity and ethics are likely to lead the way in delivering engaging, informative, and impactful multimedia journalism experiences to audiences worldwide.

Section 11.2: Predictions for the Future of Journalism

In this section, we delve into predictions for the future of journalism, considering the evolving media landscape and the role of multimedia journalism within it. Here are several key predictions:

1. Increased Integration of AI and Automation:

Prediction: AI and automation will play an integral role in news production, from generating content to aiding in data analysis and fact-checking.

Impact: This integration will enhance newsroom efficiency and enable journalists to focus more on in-depth reporting and analysis.

2. Personalization and AI-Driven Recommendations:

Prediction: News organizations will increasingly use AI algorithms to personalize content recommendations for readers, creating tailored news experiences.

Impact: Personalization will boost reader engagement and loyalty by delivering content that aligns with individual interests and preferences.

3. Augmented Reality News Experiences:

Prediction: Augmented reality (AR) will enable news consumers to access information overlaid on the physical world, enhancing understanding and context.

Impact: AR can bring data visualizations, historical context, and real-time updates directly into the reader's environment.

4. Cross-Platform Storytelling:

Prediction: Journalists will continue to adapt stories to multiple platforms, ensuring that content is accessible on various devices, including smartphones, wearables, and smart speakers.

Impact: Cross-platform storytelling will expand news organizations' reach and cater to diverse audience preferences.

5. Blockchain for Trust and Micropayments:

Prediction: Blockchain technology will be used to verify the authenticity of news sources and content, enhancing trust in journalism. Micropayments through blockchain will also provide new revenue streams for quality journalism.

Impact: Blockchain can address concerns about misinformation and enable readers to support journalism directly.

6. Virtual Reality News Reporting:

Prediction: Virtual reality (VR) will become a mainstream tool for immersive news reporting, allowing audiences to experience events as if they were on-site.

Impact: VR will provide a deeper understanding of complex stories and enhance audience engagement.

7. Voice-Activated News Services:

Prediction: News organizations will offer voice-activated news services through platforms like Amazon Alexa and Google Assistant, making news consumption more accessible and interactive.

Impact: Voice-activated news will cater to busy audiences, providing news updates and in-depth content through natural language interactions.

8. Collaborative and Crowdsourced Journalism:

Prediction: Collaborative journalism efforts and crowdsourcing will expand, involving audiences in the reporting process and verifying information.

Impact: This approach will increase the diversity of perspectives and strengthen the credibility of news stories.

9. Multimedia Training and Education:

Prediction: Multimedia journalism programs and training will evolve to include emerging technologies and new storytelling formats.

Impact: Journalists will be better equipped to navigate the evolving media landscape and deliver high-quality multimedia content.

10. Ethical Considerations and Media Literacy:

Prediction: Ethical considerations and media literacy education will be prioritized to combat misinformation and ensure responsible journalism.

Impact: Informed readers and ethical reporting will foster trust in the media and counter the spread of fake news.

The future of journalism promises both challenges and opportunities. Embracing emerging technologies while upholding journalistic principles and ethics will be crucial for news organizations and multimedia journalists to thrive in the evolving media ecosystem.

Section 11.3: Preparing for a Career in Multimedia Journalism

For individuals aspiring to pursue a career in multimedia journalism, adequate preparation is essential. This section offers guidance on how to prepare for a successful career in this dynamic field:

1. Education and Training:

Journalism Degree: Consider pursuing a bachelor's degree in journalism, communication, or a related field. Some universities also offer specialized multimedia journalism programs.

Continuous Learning: Stay updated with the latest multimedia tools and technologies through workshops, online courses, and professional development programs.

2. Build a Strong Portfolio:

Create Multimedia Content: Start building your portfolio by creating multimedia content. This could include articles, videos, podcasts, infographics, and interactive features.

Diverse Subjects: Cover a variety of subjects to showcase your versatility and range as a multimedia journalist.

3. Gain Practical Experience:

Internships: Seek internships at media organizations, newspapers, online publications, or broadcasting companies. Practical experience is invaluable for learning how newsrooms operate.

Freelancing: Consider freelancing for local publications or online platforms to gain exposure and build a network.

4. Develop Technical Skills:

Equipment Proficiency: Familiarize yourself with cameras, microphones, video editing software, and data visualization tools commonly used in multimedia journalism.

Coding Skills: Learning basic coding languages like HTML and CSS can be beneficial for creating interactive multimedia elements.

5. Stay Informed:

Current Affairs: Keep up with current events and news trends. Multimedia journalists must be well-informed about the world and various topics.

Media Trends: Follow industry publications and multimedia journalism blogs to stay updated on emerging trends and technologies.

6. Network and Collaborate:

Join Professional Organizations: Become a member of journalism associations like the Society of Professional Journalists (SPJ) or Online News Association (ONA) to network with fellow journalists.

Collaborative Projects: Collaborate with peers on multimedia projects to gain experience and learn from others.

7. Ethical Considerations:

Ethical Guidelines: Familiarize yourself with ethical guidelines and standards in journalism. Upholding ethical principles is crucial for trust and credibility.

Media Literacy: Educate yourself about media literacy and responsible reporting to combat misinformation.

8. Adaptability:

Tech Savviness: Embrace emerging technologies and be open to learning new tools and platforms as the multimedia journalism landscape evolves.

Flexibility: Be adaptable and willing to work in various formats, including text, video, audio, and interactive content.

9. Personal Branding:

Online Presence: Build an online presence through social media and a personal website or blog to showcase your work and connect with potential employers or clients.

Networking: Attend journalism conferences, webinars, and networking events to expand your professional network.

10. Internationally Focused:

Global Perspective: Develop a global perspective on news and consider covering international stories to broaden your experience.

Language Skills: Learning a second language, especially one spoken in regions of interest, can be a valuable asset.

Preparing for a career in multimedia journalism requires a combination of education, practical experience, technical skills, and a commitment to ethical reporting. By taking proactive steps to build a strong foundation and staying adaptable in the face of technological advancements, aspiring multimedia journalists can position themselves for success in this dynamic field.

Chapter 12: Conclusion

In the final chapter of this comprehensive guide on multimedia journalism, we summarize the key takeaways and offer a recap of the essential points discussed throughout the book:

Section 12.1: Recap and Key Takeaways

As we conclude this journey through the world of multimedia journalism, it's important to revisit and reflect on the key takeaways that can guide aspiring multimedia journalists and news organizations:

1. Multimedia Journalism Defined:

Multimedia journalism is a dynamic field that blends various forms of media, including text, photos, videos, audio, and interactive elements, to tell compelling and informative stories.

2. The Importance of Multimedia:

In today's digital age, multimedia elements are vital for engaging audiences and effectively conveying information. Audiences increasingly expect multimedia content.

3. Evolution of Journalism in the Digital Age:

Journalism has evolved significantly due to technological advancements, changing audience behaviors, and the rise of digital platforms. Adaptation is essential for relevance.

4. Multimedia Journalist's Toolkit:

A multimedia journalist should be proficient in using cameras, microphones, editing software, and other equipment essential for capturing and producing multimedia content.

5. Reporting Techniques:

Gathering information across platforms, conducting interviews for multimedia, and ensuring fact-checking and ethical considerations are crucial for journalistic integrity.

6. Writing for Multimedia:

Structuring multimedia news stories, crafting engaging headlines and leads, and tailoring content for different platforms are essential writing skills.

7. Visual Storytelling:

Photography in journalism, infographics, and incorporating video into stories enhance the visual appeal and impact of multimedia journalism.

8. Audio Reporting and Podcasting:

Podcasting offers a unique platform for storytelling. Recording and editing audio, along with exploring successful podcasting case studies, are valuable skills.

9. The Role of Social Media:

Social media is a powerful tool for news dissemination, but ethical considerations and personal branding are essential aspects to consider.

10. Ethics and Pitfalls:

Journalists must uphold ethical standards in multimedia reporting and be aware of common mistakes and the challenge of balancing speed and accuracy.

11. Tips for Multimedia Success:

Time management, navigating a changing media landscape, and staying updated on multimedia trends are crucial for success in the field.

12. Case Studies and Successful Organizations:

Learning from award-winning multimedia reporting projects and successful news organizations provides valuable insights into effective multimedia storytelling.

13. The Future of Multimedia Journalism:

Emerging technologies, including VR, AI, blockchain, and voice-activated news, will shape the future of multimedia journalism.

14. Preparing for a Career:

Aspiring multimedia journalists should focus on education, building a portfolio, gaining practical experience, developing technical skills, and staying informed and adaptable.

This guide has provided a comprehensive overview of multimedia journalism, from its foundational principles to its future potential. It emphasizes the importance of storytelling, ethical considerations, and adaptability in a field that continues to evolve. As you embark on your journey in multimedia journalism, remember that your dedication to truth, innovation, and audience engagement will be your most powerful assets. Keep learning, stay curious, and continue to push the boundaries of multimedia journalism to inform, inspire, and make a difference in the world of news and storytelling.

Section 12.2: Encouraging the Next Generation of Multimedia Journalists

In Section 12.2, we focus on the importance of nurturing and supporting the next generation of multimedia journalists. Encouraging and guiding aspiring journalists is vital for the continued growth and innovation of the field. Here are key points to consider:

1. Mentorship and Education:

Encourage experienced multimedia journalists to serve as mentors for aspiring journalists. Mentorship programs provide valuable guidance and insights.

Advocate for journalism education programs that emphasize multimedia skills. Encourage universities and institutions to offer courses and workshops tailored to the demands of modern journalism.

2. Accessible Resources:

Promote the availability of affordable or free resources for learning multimedia journalism. Online courses, tutorials, and open-source software can help aspiring journalists build their skills.

Encourage news organizations to offer internships, apprenticeships, and training programs that provide hands-on experience in multimedia reporting.

3. Embrace Diversity and Inclusion:

Advocate for diversity and inclusion in newsrooms and journalism education. A diverse group of voices and perspectives strengthens journalism as a whole.

Support initiatives that provide opportunities for underrepresented groups in journalism, such as scholarships and mentorship programs.

4. Ethics and Media Literacy:

Promote media literacy education to equip the public with critical thinking skills to discern reliable news sources from misinformation.

Encourage discussions and workshops on journalistic ethics to ensure the next generation of journalists upholds high standards of integrity and responsibility.

5. Collaboration and Innovation:

Foster a culture of collaboration between experienced journalists and emerging talent. Joint projects can help bridge the generation gap and encourage innovation.

Support initiatives that promote innovation in journalism, such as hackathons or grants for multimedia journalism startups.

6. Adaptation to Changing Landscape:

Encourage flexibility and adaptability in the face of changing technologies and audience preferences. Aspiring journalists should be prepared to embrace emerging tools and platforms.

Highlight the importance of lifelong learning and staying updated on industry trends. Conferences, webinars, and industry events provide opportunities for growth.

7. Recognize Achievements:

Celebrate and recognize the achievements of emerging multimedia journalists through awards, competitions, and showcases. This recognition can motivate and inspire the next generation.

Encourage news organizations to provide platforms for young journalists to showcase their work and gain visibility.

8. Encourage Civic Engagement:

Advocate for journalism that promotes civic engagement and social responsibility. Encourage aspiring journalists to cover issues that have a positive impact on their communities.

Support initiatives that promote investigative journalism and hold those in power accountable.

By actively encouraging the next generation of multimedia journalists, we can ensure that the field continues to evolve, adapt, and thrive. Nurturing talent, fostering a commitment to ethical journalism, and embracing innovation will contribute to a vibrant and impactful future for multimedia journalism.

Appendices

In the appendices section, you can find additional resources and information to complement your journey in multimedia journalism. These appendices offer practical tools, references, and further reading to enhance your understanding and skills:

Appendix A: Multimedia Journalism Resources

1. Recommended Reading: A curated list of books, articles, and research papers that delve into various aspects of multimedia journalism, including storytelling techniques, ethics, and emerging technologies.

2. Online Courses: Links to reputable online courses and platforms where you can enhance your multimedia journalism skills, often at your own pace.

3. Software and Tools: A list of essential software and tools used in multimedia journalism, along with links to download or access them.

4. Professional Organizations: Information about journalism associations and professional organizations that offer networking opportunities, conferences, and resources for multimedia journalists.

Appendix B: Ethical Guidelines for Multimedia Journalism

1. Code of Ethics: A comprehensive overview of ethical guidelines and principles that should be upheld in multimedia journalism, including accuracy, fairness, and responsible reporting.

2. Case Studies: Real-world case studies illustrating ethical dilemmas and how they were addressed in multimedia journalism projects.

Appendix C: Glossary of Multimedia Journalism Terms

1. Key Terms: Definitions and explanations of multimedia journalism terminology, ensuring clarity and understanding of industry-specific terms.

Appendix D: Sample Multimedia Journalism Projects

1. Interactive Features: Links to interactive multimedia journalism projects that showcase innovative storytelling techniques and engagement with audiences.

2. Video Reporting: Examples of video reports and documentaries that demonstrate the power of visual storytelling.

3. Podcasts: Links to compelling news podcasts that highlight the diversity of content and styles in audio journalism.

Appendix E: Multimedia Journalism Toolkit

1. Equipment Checklist: A checklist of essential equipment for multimedia journalists, including cameras, microphones, and accessories.

2. Software and Apps: A list of recommended software and mobile apps for capturing, editing, and producing multimedia content.

Appendix F: Further Reading on Emerging Technologies

1. Emerging Technologies in Journalism: Additional reading and resources on emerging technologies such as virtual reality, artificial intelligence, and blockchain in journalism.

Appendix G: Multimedia Journalism Competitions and Awards

1. Notable Competitions: A list of prestigious multimedia journalism competitions and awards that offer recognition and opportunities for emerging talent.

Appendix H: Journalism Scholarships and Grants

1. Scholarships: Information about scholarships and grants available to support aspiring multimedia journalists in their education and career development.

Appendix I: References

1. Citations: A comprehensive list of sources and references used throughout this guide, providing a basis for further research and exploration.

These appendices are designed to be a valuable resource for multimedia journalists, educators, and anyone interested in the field of multimedia journalism. Whether you're looking for additional reading material, ethical guidance, or practical tools, these appendices aim to enrich your multimedia journalism journey.

Appendix A: Glossary of Multimedia Journalism Terms

This glossary provides definitions and explanations of key terms commonly used in the field of multimedia journalism. Understanding these terms is essential for effective communication and collaboration in the world of multimedia reporting:

1. Multimedia Journalism: Journalism that incorporates various forms of media, such as text, photos, videos, audio, and interactive elements, to tell stories and convey information.

2. Interactive Feature: Multimedia content that allows users to actively engage with and explore the story, often through interactive graphics, animations, or clickable elements.

3. Data Visualization: The presentation of data in a visual format, such as charts, graphs, and infographics, to make complex information more accessible and understandable.

4. Infographic: A visual representation of information, data, or statistics, often using icons, charts, and diagrams to convey a message concisely.

5. User-Generated Content (UGC): Content, such as photos, videos, or comments, created and shared by the audience or users of a media platform.

6. Podcast: A digital audio program that can cover a wide range of topics, including news, storytelling, interviews, and discussions.

7. Livestreaming: Broadcasting live video or audio content over the internet in real-time, allowing viewers to watch events as they happen.

8. Parallax Scrolling: A web design technique where different layers of content move at different speeds as the user scrolls, creating a 3D effect and enhancing storytelling.

9. B-roll: Supplementary footage or video clips used to provide context, visuals, or transitions in a video report.

10. Anchor: A multimedia journalist or presenter who hosts a news program, often delivering headlines and introducing segments.

11. Vox Populi: A Latin term meaning "voice of the people." In journalism, it refers to collecting opinions and comments from the public on a specific topic or issue.

12. Dateline: A line at the beginning of a news article or report that indicates the location and date of the story's origin.

13. Byline: The author's name, often accompanied by a photograph, at the beginning or end of an article, indicating the writer of the piece.

14. Copyediting: The process of reviewing and editing written content for clarity, grammar, spelling, and style before publication.

15. Multimedia Storytelling: The practice of using various media formats, such as text, images, audio, and video, to convey a narrative or story.

16. Embed: To incorporate or insert multimedia elements, such as videos or social media posts, directly into a web page or article.

17. Transparency: The practice of being open and honest about the sources, methods, and processes used in multimedia journalism, promoting trust and credibility.

18. Attribution: Giving proper credit to the original source or creator of multimedia content, such as images, videos, or quotes, used in a journalistic report.

19. Ethics: The moral principles and standards that guide ethical decision-making and behavior in journalism, including accuracy, fairness, and accountability.

20. Mobile Journalism (MoJo): The practice of producing multimedia journalism content using smartphones or mobile devices, often for on-the-go reporting.

21. 360-Degree Video: Video footage that captures a panoramic view in all directions, allowing viewers to control their perspective and immerse themselves in the scene.

22. Live Blogging: The real-time reporting of events, updates, or developments on a blog or website, often accompanied by multimedia elements.

23. Crowdsourcing: The practice of soliciting input, information, or contributions from a large group of people, often the audience or online community.

24. Lead: The opening sentence or paragraph of a news article that summarizes the most important information and entices the reader to continue reading.

25. Multimedia Newsroom: A newsroom equipped with the necessary tools and technology to produce multimedia content, including cameras, microphones, and video editing software.

26. Storyboard: A visual outline or plan that depicts the sequence of scenes or elements in a multimedia story, often used in video production.

27. Caption: A brief description or explanation accompanying a photo or image, providing context and information to the viewer.

28. Viral Content: Multimedia content, such as videos or articles, that spreads rapidly and widely across the internet, often through social media sharing.

29. Drone Journalism: The use of unmanned aerial vehicles (drones) to capture aerial footage and images for journalistic purposes.

30. Content Management System (CMS): Software or platforms used to create, edit, organize, and publish multimedia content on websites and digital platforms.

This glossary serves as a reference for multimedia journalists, educators, and enthusiasts, offering clarity on the terminology essential to the practice of multimedia journalism.

Appendix B: Recommended Resources and Further Reading

This appendix provides a curated list of recommended resources and further reading materials for multimedia journalists, educators, and those interested in expanding their knowledge of multimedia journalism. These resources cover a range of topics, from storytelling techniques to ethics and emerging technologies:

1. Books on Multimedia Journalism:

"The Multimedia Journalist: Storytelling for Today's Media Landscape" by Jennifer George-Palilonis

"Multimedia Storytelling for Digital Communicators in a Multiplatform World" by Seth Gitner

"The Data Journalism Handbook" edited by Jonathan Gray, Liliana Bounegru, and Lucy Chambers

2. Online Courses and Training:

Poynter's News University (www.poynter.org/newsu): Offers a variety of online courses on multimedia journalism topics, including video production and data visualization.

Coursera (www.coursera.org): Features courses on multimedia storytelling, photography, and video production from universities and institutions worldwide.

3. Journalism Organizations and Associations:

Society of Professional Journalists (SPJ) (www.spj.org): Provides resources, ethical guidelines, and networking opportunities for journalists.

Online News Association (ONA) (www.ona.org): Focuses on digital journalism and offers conferences, training, and resources for multimedia journalists.

4. Multimedia Reporting Tools and Software:

Adobe Creative Cloud (www.adobe.com/creativecloud): Includes essential software for multimedia journalism, such as Adobe Premiere Pro, Photoshop, and Audition.

Datawrapper (www.datawrapper.de): A user-friendly tool for creating interactive charts and maps for data-driven stories.

5. Ethical Journalism Guidelines:

The Society of Professional Journalists' Code of Ethics (www.spj.org/ethicscode.asp) outlines the principles and standards of ethical journalism.

The Reuters Handbook of Journalism (www.handbook.reuters.com) offers guidelines for ethical reporting and multimedia journalism practices.

6. Multimedia Storytelling Platforms:

StoryMapJS (https://storymap.knightlab.com): A user-friendly tool for creating interactive maps and multimedia narratives.

TimelineJS (https://timeline.knightlab.com): Enables the creation of interactive timelines with multimedia elements.

7. Blogs and Multimedia Journalism Platforms:

Nieman Journalism Lab (www.niemanlab.org): Offers insights and analysis on multimedia journalism trends and innovations.

NPR Visuals (https://apps.npr.org/visuals): Showcases award-winning multimedia journalism projects and storytelling techniques.

8. Media Literacy and Fact-Checking:

Media Literacy Now (www.medialiteracynow.org): Provides resources and advocacy for media literacy education.

International Fact-Checking Network (www.poynter.org/ifcn): Offers fact-checking resources and a directory of fact-checking organizations worldwide.

9. Emerging Technologies in Journalism:

"Journalism 360" (https://journalism360.com): Explores the intersection of journalism and immersive technologies like virtual reality and augmented reality.

The Knight Foundation's "AI in Journalism Playbook" (https://aiplaybook.aipolicy.xyz): Discusses the use of artificial intelligence in journalism.

10. Podcasts on Journalism and Storytelling:

"The Journalist's Toolbox Podcast" (www.journaliststoolbox.org/podcast): Features discussions on multimedia journalism tools and techniques.

"Longform Podcast" (www.longform.org/podcast): Interviews with journalists, including multimedia practitioners, about their work and processes.

These resources offer valuable insights, tools, and guidance for multimedia journalists as they navigate the ever-evolving landscape of journalism. Whether you're a seasoned professional or just beginning your journey, exploring these materials can enhance your skills and understanding of multimedia storytelling.

Appendix C: Sample Multimedia News Stories

In this appendix, you will find links to sample multimedia news stories that exemplify effective storytelling across various formats and platforms. These stories showcase the power of multimedia journalism to engage audiences and convey important information:

1. "Snowfall: The Avalanche at Tunnel Creek" (The New York Times)

Link: Snowfall - The New York Times

Description: This Pulitzer Prize-winning multimedia story combines text, photos, videos, and interactive graphics to narrate the harrowing events of an avalanche. It's a prime example of immersive storytelling.

2. "A Year at War" (Los Angeles Times)

Link: A Year at War - Los Angeles Times

Description: This series of multimedia reports follows a platoon of soldiers deployed in Afghanistan. It incorporates text, photos, videos, and interactive elements to provide a comprehensive view of their experiences.

3. "Firestorm" (The Guardian)

Link: Firestorm - The Guardian

Description: This interactive feature uses maps, data visualizations, and photos to explain the devastating bushfires in Australia, offering a clear picture of how the fires spread.

4. "The Daily" Podcast (The New York Times)

Link: The Daily - The New York Times

Description: "The Daily" is a podcast that provides in-depth analysis of top news stories through interviews, audio clips, and storytelling. It's an excellent example of audio journalism.

5. "Planet Money Makes a T-shirt" (NPR)

Link: Planet Money Makes a T-shirt - NPR

Description: This multimedia project takes you on a journey to understand the global supply chain of a simple T-shirt, combining audio, text, photos, and interactive elements.

6. "The Dark Side of Japan's Olympics" (BBC News)

Link: The Dark Side of Japan's Olympics - BBC News

Description: This investigative multimedia report utilizes video, text, images, and data to uncover the human rights issues surrounding the Tokyo Olympics.

7. "The New American Slavery: Invited to the U.S., Foreign Workers Find a Nightmare" (Reveal from The Center for Investigative Reporting)

Link: The New American Slavery - Reveal

Description: This multimedia investigation combines written articles, audio segments, and interactive elements to expose labor exploitation in the United States.

8. "The Displaced" (The New York Times)

Link: The Displaced - The New York Times

Description: This virtual reality project follows the lives of three refugee children through immersive 360-degree videos, providing a unique storytelling experience.

These sample multimedia news stories offer a glimpse into the diverse range of storytelling techniques and formats used in journalism today. Explore them to gain inspiration and insight into how multimedia can be effectively harnessed to inform and engage audiences.

About Author

Osman Karakas is an accomplished journalist, editor, researcher, photographer, and author with a diverse and extensive background in the field of journalism. With a passion for storytelling and a commitment to journalistic integrity, Osman Karakas has made significant contributions to the media industry throughout his career.

Osman Karakas has been recognized for his outstanding work and has received numerous awards and accolades. In 1991, he was honored with the Excellence in Journalism award by the Deadline Club-Society of Professional Journalists in New York, USA.

In 1990, Osman Karakas won first place in the Spot News category at the Associated Press Association, New York, for his impactful news story titled "Don't Let Him Die" published in the New York Post.

He also received the prestigious Picture of the Year Award in 1990 from the University of Missouri - School of Journalism/National Press Photographers Association, his photography was compared to Michelangelo's "Pieta" by the head of the jury.

His international experience continued as they worked as a correspondent at the United Nations for Anadolu Weekly in New York, USA, and later as a Correspondent and News & Photo Editor for Hurriyet International Daily, covering press conferences at the UN.

In addition to his international assignments, Osman Karakas his career in journalism as a correspondent for TRT (Turkish Radio & Television) in Turkmenistan and Kazakhstan from 1993 to 1996. During this time, they also served as the Editor-in-Chief of the TURKCAN International Magazine in Turkmenistan. Also manager and editor-in-Chief various newspapers and magazines in Türkiye and Central Asia.

Osman Karakas has been involved in academia as well, having worked as a Lecturer at Manas University in Bishkek, Kyrgyzstan, where they taught journalism courses, advised students, and served on various committees about 8 years. His dedication to education and knowledge sharing has been instrumental in nurturing the next generation of journalists.

With proficiency in multiple languages, including English, Turkish, Russian, Turkmen, Azerbaijan, Kyrgyz, and Kazakh, Osman Karakas has been able to communicate and report on diverse topics with cultural sensitivity and understanding. his language skills have allowed them to engage with various communities and provide insightful coverage.

Alongside his journalistic career, Osman Karakas has authored several books and documentaries, covering topics ranging from journalism to detective novels and documentaries on historical events. They have also exhibited his photography in multiple personal exhibitions in Turkey and Kyrgyzstan, showcasing his artistic talent and unique perspective.

Osman Karakas possesses a wide range of skills and expertise, including diplomacy, media relations, public relations, political campaign management, managing media, photography, communication, and web publishing. Including; advertising, social media, and desktop publishing, keeping up with the evolving landscape of digital journalism.

In conclusion, Osman Karakas has made significant contributions to the field of journalism through his exceptional work, awards, publications, and dedication to journalistic ethics. His diverse experiences, international exposure, and commitment to storytelling have shaped his career and established them as a respected figure in the media industry.

Recommended Books

The Complete Guide to
INVESTIGATIVE
JOURNALISM
A Handbook for Candidate and
New - Beginner Journalists
OSMAN KARAKAS
Award-winning Journalist & Lecturer

A COMPREHENSIVE AND
PRACTICAL GUIDEBOOK
News Writing
Techniques
MOST COMMON MISTAKES AND TIPS
OSMAN KARAKAS
AWARD-WINNING JOURNALIST & LECTURER

PROFESSIONAL
PHOTO
JOURNALISM
NEW YORK POST
'Don't let
him die!'
A Comprehensive Study Guide
for Professional Journalists
OSMAN KARAKAS
Award-winning Journalist & Lecturer

THE SOCIAL
MEDIA
PARADOX
Citizen Journalism or
Social Media Terror?
OSMAN KARAKAS
AWARD-WINNING JOURNALIST & LECTURER

PEACEFUL AND EFFECIVE
INTERNATIONAL RELATIONS
BUILDING
BRIDGES
NAVIGATING DIPLOMACY
COOPERATION AND
GLOBAL PROGRESS
OSMAN KARAKAS
AWARD-WINNING JOURNALIST & LECTURER

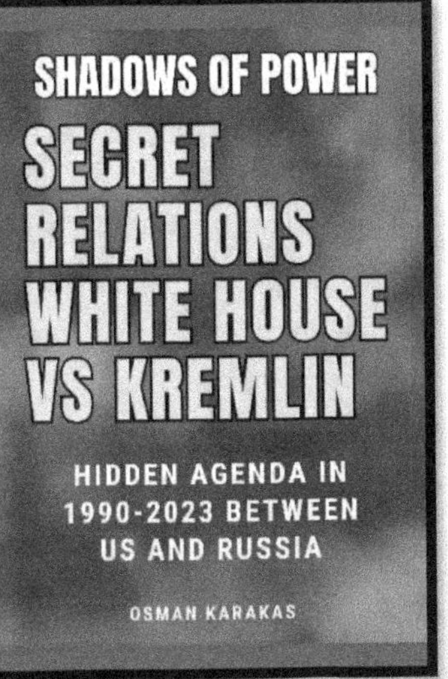
SHADOWS OF POWER
SECRET
RELATIONS
WHITE HOUSE
VS KREMLIN
HIDDEN AGENDA IN
1990-2023 BETWEEN
US AND RUSSIA
OSMAN KARAKAS

COMPREHENSIVE GUIDE THAT EXPLORES THE
INTRICATE WORLD OF CRISIS DIPLOMACY
ART OF
DIPLOMACY
IN CRISES
NAVIGATING INTERNATIONAL
RELATIONS WITH FINESSE AND
STRATEGIC EXCELLENCE
OSMAN KARAKAS

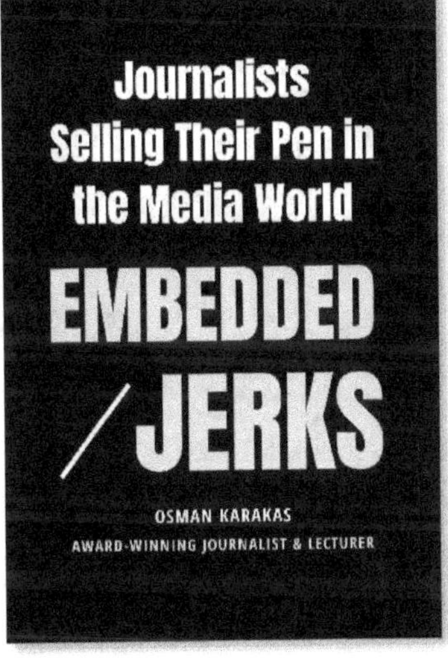
Journalists
Selling Their Pen in
the Media World
EMBEDDED
/ JERKS
OSMAN KARAKAS
AWARD-WINNING JOURNALIST & LECTURER

THE DARK
UNDERBELLY
Unmasking the Secrets of
Entertainment Programs
Exposing Manipulation,
Scandals and the Price of Fame
in Show Business
OSMAN KARAKAS

MANIPULATION
OF MEDIA
NEWS
THE EROSION OF REALITY IN THE
MODERN NEWS LANDSCAPE
OSMAN KARAKAS
AWARD-WINNING JOURNALIST & LECTURER

INTERNATIONAL
JOURNALISM
Global Perspectives of
International News
OSMAN KARAKAS
AWARD-WINNING JOURNALIST & LECTURER

An Easy-to-Digest Exploration
of Africa's Complex Realities
The Dark
Destiny
of
AFRICA
Navigating Challenges, Forging Hope
OSMAN KARAKAS

The collection of books is accessible for purchase on Amazon.com platform.